Company logotype 1926, Tempelhof Airport Berlin.

Take-off and landing at Berlin's Tegel Airport.

Berlin, Berlin.

No city's ties with Lufthansa have a more chequered history than those of Berlin. The City was the prewar hub of the airline's route network following the founding there of Lufthansa's predecessor Luft Hansa in 1926. After 1945, the political situation barred the reborn Lufthansa from flying to Berlin again until 1990. Meantime, the City has regained its status as a major destination in the Lufthansa timetable: The airline now operates 600 flights weekly to the capital from German airports. Change in the City has been just as rapid as the growth in its air traffic. Berlin is truly a City of the future, and Lufthansa and its subsidiaries are again making a contribution. More than 3,500 people are now in their employ in the City on the Spree.

A visit to Berlin anytime will not disappoint. Ask the soccer fans chanting "we're off to Berlin" on their way to the German cup final staged in the City yearly. But if you're going, why not fly? On any of Lufthansa's daily flights to Berlin at very attractive fares. All the details on those flights as well as others Lufthansa operates to more than 190 destinations around the globe are readily available at www.lufthansa.com. There's no better way to fly.

A STAR ALLIANCE MEMBER ✪

COOL
Berlin

teNeues

Imprint

Editors: Martin Nicholas Kunz, Editorial coordination: Lea Bauer

Photos (location): © Lafayette Presseabteilung, Berlin (Galeries Lafayette Berlin, p. 7 b. l.), Agentur GRACO (berlinomat), Anette Kiesling (Bar Tausend, p. 13), arena Berlin (BADESCHIFF an der arena Berlin, p. 5 b. r.), Armin von Hodenberg (Rooms Interior GmbH), © courtesy Telekom Shop Vertriebsgesellschaft mbH/Andreas Meichsner (4010 – Der Telekom Shop in Mitte), © Adlon Holding GmbH (MA Restaurant), © Alpenstueck (Alpenstueck, p. 7 b. r.), © Bonanza Coffee Heroes (Bonanza Coffee Heroes), © Brauer Photos (Mercedes-Benz Fashion Week), © bullet event gmbh (Weekend, p. 10), © Café Einstein Stammhaus (Café Einstein Stammhaus), © Camera Work (Galerie CAMERA WORK, Museum THE KENNEDYS), Claus Rasmussen for Herr von Eden (Herr von Eden), © Cookies Cream (Cookies Cream, p. 12 b. l.), © Departmentstore Quartier 206 (Departmentstore Quartier 206), © RENÉ LEZARD Mode GmbH (RENÉ LEZARD Shop Berlin Mitte, p. 10 b. l.), © Rooms (Rooms Interior GmbH), © Solar / Ragnar Schmuck (Solar), diephotodesigner.de (Il Calice, Spindler & Klatt, Green Door, pp. 3, 4 b. r., 8 b. l.), Eisenhart Keimeyer (Anna Blume, Bocca di Bacco, Bonanza Coffee Heroes, Vienna Bar, DC4 &JOHN DE MAYA PROJECT, lucid21, Nanna Kuckuck, Shan Rahimkhan, Vintage-Sunglasses.de + OptiKing, 12 b. r.), Gavin Jackson (blush Dessous, BADESCHIFF an der arena Berlin), © keller-fotografie.de (Mercedes-Benz Gallery), Ivan Nemec (Il Calice), Jörg Tietje (Adnan, Borchardt, Kuchi, p. 4 b. l.), M. Mettel Siefen (BADESCHIFF an der arena Berlin, p. 178), Markus Bachmann (Fiona Bennett Salon, pp. 8 b. r., 102), Martin Nicholas Kunz (Berliner Ensemble, East Side Gallery, Hackescher Markt, Kino International, pp. 6, 10 b. r.), Michelle Galindo (Berliner Ensemble, Hackescher Markt), Rainer Klostermeier (Bar 103), Stefan Korte (Grill Royal, p. 14), Stephan Schmidt (bob – boxoffberlin), Yves Sucksdorff, Berlin (Berlinomat, p. 5 b. l.)

Cover photo (location): Borchardt (Jörg Tietje, www.fusion-publishing.com)

Back cover photos from top to bottom (location): diephotodesigner.de (Il Calice), © Adlon Holding GmbH (MA Restaurant), Eisenhart Keimeyer (Shan Rahimkhan)

Price categories: € = reasonable, €€ = moderate, €€€ = upscale, €€€€ = expensive

Introduction, Texts: Raphael Guillou, Layout & Pre-press, Imaging: fusion publishing, Translations: Übersetzungsbüro RR Communications: English: Robert Rosenbaum, Christie Tam; French: Laure Buchaillard, Félicien Guebane; Spanish: Pablo Álvarez, Bruno Plaza

Produced by fusion publishing GmbH, Berlin   www.fusion-publishing.com

Published by teNeues Publishing Group

teNeues Verlag GmbH + Co. KG
Am Selder 37
47906 Kempen, Germany
Tel.: 0049-(0)2152-916-0
Fax: 0049-(0)2152-916-111
E-mail: books@teneues.de

teNeues Publishing Company
16 West 22nd Street
New York, NY 10010, USA
Tel.: 001-212-627-9090
Fax: 001-212-627-9511

teNeues Publishing UK Ltd.
21 Marlowe Court, Lymer Avenue
London SE19 1LP, Great Britain
Phone: 0044-208-670-7522
Fax: 0044-208-670-7523

Press department:
arehn@teneues.de
Tel.: 0049-2152-916-202

teNeues France S.A.R.L.
39, rue des Billets
18250 Henrichemont, France
Phone: 0033-2-4826-9348
Fax: 0033-1-7072-3482

www.teneues.com

ISBN: 978-3-8327-9400-2

© 2010 teNeues Verlag GmbH + Co. KG, Kempen

Printed in Italy

Bibliographic information published by the Deutsche Nationalbibliothek.

The Deutsche Nationalbibliothek lists this publication in the Deutsche Nationalbibliografie; detailed bibliographic data are available in the Internet at http://dnb.d-nb.de.

RESTAURANTS & CAFÉS

CLUBS, LOUNGES & BARS

SHOPS

HIGHLIGHTS

SERVICE

Introduction

Whenever Berlin is mentioned outside Germany, the first thing you hear is, "I love Berlin! I want to go there!"

No one has forgotten that an impenetrable wall once divided the German capital into East and West, but the will of the younger and older generations to put that period behind them and turn Berlin back into a vibrant world-class city can be seen and felt all around. The relatively inexpensive housing and cost of living attract young artists and designers from all corners of the globe. They come to live and work in the multicultural atmosphere, drawing important events in their wake such as the Berlin Biennal and Fashion Week. That's not the only reason Berlin's cultural calendar can stand up to comparison. The same goes for urban design since the city's reunification. Today the city's appearance is shaped by numerous futuristic buildings by renowned architects, in addition to lovingly restored historic locations and monuments like the new Holocaust memorial. And because new shops, restaurants, and bars are opening up every day, the German capital can hold its own against any city in the world when it comes to nightlife. After dinner in a first-class restaurant like "MĂ Restaurant" and drinks at the "Bar Tausend" or the "Green Door," night owls can easily find their favorite clubs where they can party till dawn, ideally with a view of the TV tower, as is available at "Weekend."

Some aficionados compare Berlin to the New York of the wild '80s. One thing is certain: Berlin has developed into a world-class metropolis!

Raphael Guillou

Einleitung

Sobald im Ausland die Rede von Berlin ist, bekommt man immer wieder zu hören „I love Berlin! I want to go there!"

Dass eine unüberwindbare Mauer die Bundeshauptstadt einst in West und Ost teilte, ist keineswegs vergessen, aber der Wille der jungen und alten Generation, diese Zeit hinter sich zu lassen und Berlin zu einer brodelnden Weltstadt zu machen, ist überall spür- und sichtbar. Vergleichsweise günstige Miet- und Lebenshaltungskosten ziehen junge Künstler und Designer aus aller Welt an. Sie kommen, um in der multikulturellen Atmosphäre zu leben und zu arbeiten, und sie ziehen wichtige Veranstaltungen wie die „Berlin Biennale" und die „Fashion Week" nach sich. Nicht zuletzt deshalb kann sich das Kulturangebot Berlins sehen lassen. Das gilt auch für den Städtebau nach der Wende. Heute prägen neben liebevoll restaurierten geschichtsträchtigen Orten und Gedenkstätten wie dem neuen Holocaust-Denkmal vielfach futuristische Gebäude namhafter Architekten das Stadtbild. Und da täglich neue Läden, Restaurants, Bars eröffnen, muss die deutsche Hauptstadt auch in punkto Nachtleben keinen internationalen Vergleich scheuen. Nach dem Dinner in einem First Class Restaurant wie dem „MÄ Restaurant" und einigen Drinks in der „Bar Tausend" oder im „Green Door" findet jeder Nachtschwärmer leicht „seinen" Club, um bis in die Morgenstunden zu feiern, am Besten mit Blick auf den Fernsehturm wie im „Weekend".

Mancher Kenner vergleicht Berlin mit dem New York der wilden 80er-Jahre. Eines ist ganz sicher: Berlin hat sich zur Weltmetropole entwickelt!

Raphael Guillou

Introduction

À l'étranger, dès qu'il est question de Berlin, on n'en finit plus d'entendre : « J'aime Berlin ! J'aime aller à Berlin ! ».

Si le mur infranchissable qui autrefois divisait la capitale fédérale en deux parties est bien présent dans les esprits, la volonté de l'ancienne comme de la nouvelle génération de clore définitivement ce chapitre pour faire de Berlin une grande ville bouillonnante de renommée mondiale est, elle aussi, partout perceptible et visible. Le coût de la vie et les prix de location relativement abordables attirent jeunes créateurs et artistes des quatre coins du globe. Ils viennent à Berlin pour vivre et travailler dans une ambiance multiculturelle et d'importantes manifestations telles que la « Biennale de Berlin » et la « Fashion Week » voient le jour avec eux. C'est également pour cela que l'offre culturelle de Berlin n'a rien à envier à celle d'autres métropoles, tout comme l'urbanisme après le tournant de 1989. Aujourd'hui, des bâtiments pour la plupart futuristes signés par de prestigieux architectes côtoyant des lieux chargés d'histoire et minutieusement restaurés et des monuments, tels que le nouveau Mémorial de l'Holocauste, s'inscrivent dans le paysage urbain. De nouveaux magasins, restaurants et bars poussant comme des champignons, la capitale allemande peut également faire jeu égal avec d'autres métropoles en ce qui concerne la vie nocturne. Après avoir dîné dans un restaurant de premier ordre comme le « MÃ Restaurant » et pris un verre au bar « Tausend » ou « Green Door », chaque noctambule y trouvera *club à son pied* et pourra s'amuser jusqu'au petit matin avec en prime une vue panoramique sur la célèbre « Fernsehturm » offerte, par exemple, depuis le night-club « Weekend ».

Certains connaisseurs comparent Berlin avec le New York endiablé des années 80. Une chose est sûre : Berlin est devenue LA métropole mondiale !

Raphael Guillou

Introducción

Siempre que se habla de Berlín fuera de Alemania, antes o después hay alguien que comenta: "¡Me encanta Berlín! ¡Cómo me gustaría ir!".

Nadie olvida que en otra época un muro infranqueable dividía el este y el oeste de la ciudad; hoy, sin embargo, resulta palpable la determinación de las antiguas y las nuevas generaciones por superar aquel pasado y hacer de Berlín una vibrante y moderna metrópoli. El reducido precio de los alquileres y un coste de vida relativamente asequible atraen a artistas y diseñadores de todo el mundo. Acuden a la ciudad en busca de una atmósfera multicultural en la que vivir y trabajar, y traen consigo eventos de gran calibre como la Biennale y la *Fashion Week*. Por este y otros muchos motivos la oferta cultural de Berlín resiste cualquier comparación internacional. Lo mismo puede decirse de la proyección urbanística de la capital tras la caída del Muro. La imagen actual de la ciudad está marcada por la cuidadosa restauración de numerosos edificios cargados de historia y monumentos como el dedicado a la memoria de las víctimas del Holocausto, pero también por los edificios futuristas de arquitectos de renombre internacional. Cada día se inauguran en la ciudad nuevas tiendas, nuevos restaurantes, nuevos bares: la vida nocturna berlinesa no tiene nada que envidiar a la de otras grandes capitales. Tras cenar en un restaurante de campanillas como "MÃ Restaurant" y un par de copas en "Bar Tausend" o "Green Door", los noctámbulos acabarán encontrando un local a su medida en el que continuar la fiesta hasta la madrugada, quizá con vistas a la torre de televisión, como en Weekend.

Voces autorizadas comparan Berlín con el Nueva York de los desmadrados años ochenta. Una cosa es segura: Berlín ha mutado para convertirse en una de las principales metrópolis del mundo.

Raphael Guillou

Museum THE KENNEDYS

Pariser Platz 4a
10117 Berlin
Mitte
Phone: +49 / 30 / 20 65 35 70
www.thekennedys.de

Opening hours: Daily 10 am to 6 pm
Public transportation: U, S Brandenburger Tor
Map: No. 44

The Museum THE KENNEDYS boasts one of the world's most extensive exhibitions of Kennedy family history. The roughly 300 exhibits come from the collection of Camera Work AG, and were selected with the help of scholars from the John F. Kennedy Institute at the Free University of Berlin. With photographs, documents, and personal objects, supplemented with didactic and media resources, the museum presents an intimate homage to what is likely the most famous family in American politics.

Das Museum THE KENNEDYS zeigt eine der weltweit umfangreichsten Ausstellungen zur Familienge-schichte der Kennedys. Die rund 300 Exponate entstammen der Sammlung der Camera Work AG und wurden mit Hilfe von Wissenschaftlern aus dem John-F.-Kennedy-Institut der Freien Universität Berlin ausgewählt. Durch Fotos, Dokumente und private Gegenstände, ergänzt durch didaktische und mediale Mittel, ist eine intime Hommage an die wohl bekannteste Familie der amerikanischen Politik entstanden.

Le musée THE KENNEDYS abrite l'une des expositions les plus complètes au monde consacrée à l'histoire de la famille Kennedy. Les quelque 300 pièces proviennent de la collection de la société Camera Work AG et ont été sélectionnées en collaboration avec des scientifiques de l'Institut John F. Kennedy de la Freie Uni-versität Berlin. Photos, documents et objets personnels, complétés par des moyens didactiques et médiati-ques, permettent de rendre un hommage intime à la famille la plus célèbre de la scène politique américaine.

El museo THE KENNEDYS acoge una de las exposiciones más completas en todo el mundo dedicada a la historia familiar de los Kennedy. Los cerca de 300 objetos expuestos proceden de la colección Camera Work AG y han sido seleccionados con ayuda de expertos del Instituto John F. Kennedy de la Universidad Libre de Berlín. A través de fotografías, documentos y objetos personales, complementados con diversos medios didácticos, aparece ante el visitante un íntimo homenaje a la que posiblemente sea la familia más famosa de la política estadounidense.

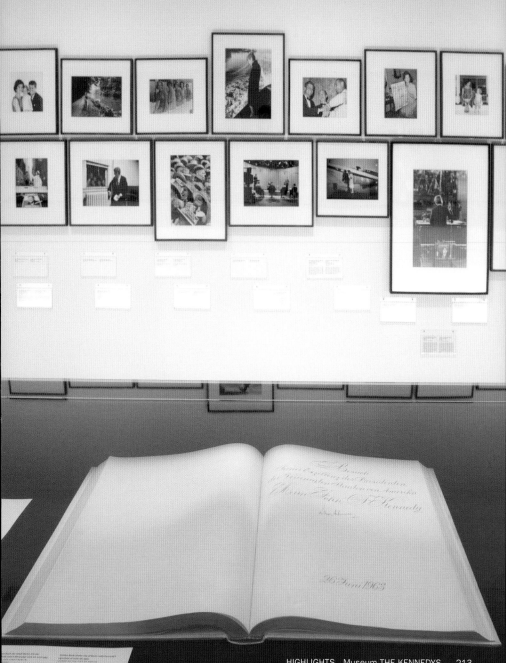

ARRIVING IN BERLIN

By plane

Information on airports and current security regulations: Phone: +49 (0)1 80 / 5 00 01 86 (12 ct/min.) www.berlin-airport.de

Schönefeld Airport (SXF)

Located about 11 miles south of the city center. National and international flights. Free shuttle service or 5–10 min walk from terminal to train station. For city center, take S9, Regionalbahn or Airport Express to Friedrichstraße or Zoologischer Garten. The trip takes 30–45 min. Alternatively, take bus no. 171 from the terminal to Rudow subway station (U7). Taxis to City West or City East take approximately 30 min and cost about 23 €.

Tegel Airport (TXL)

Located about 5 miles north-west of the city center. National and international flights. Take bus no. 128 from terminal to Kurt-Schumacher-Platz subway station. Take U6 subway to Friedrichstraße. The trip takes 30 min. Alternatively, take bus no. 109 or express bus X9 to Zoologischer Garten (via Jakob-Kaiser-Platz U7 subway station), 20–30 min. journey. Or take TXL Express-Bus to Alexanderplatz (via Hauptbahnhof and Friedrichstraße), around 35 min. journey. Taxis to City West / City East take approximately 15/25 min and cost 15 €/17 €.

Tempelhof Airport (THF)

Located just south of the city center. Predominantly national flights. Take U6 subway for direct connection to city center, 10–20 min trip. Taxis to City West or City East take 10–15 min and cost around 12 €. Berlin Tempelhof Airport will discontinue operation as soon as construction of the new Berlin-Brandenburg International Airport is completed.

By train

Berliner Hauptbahnhof

Europaplatz 1
www.hbf-berlin.de
Berlin's magnificent new Central Train Station is located close to the new city center and the Reichstag. Direct connection to local lines S5, S7, S9 and S75.

Further information

Phone: +49 (0)8 00 / 1 50 70 90 (automatic timetable information)
Phone: +49 (0)118 61 (travel service)
www.bahn.de

INFORMATION

Tourist information

Berlin Tourismus Marketing (BTM)

Am Karlsbad 11
10785 Berlin
Phone: +49 (0)30 / 25 00 25
Fax: +49 (0)30 / 25 00 24 24
www.btm.de
information@btm.de (to order information material)
reservierung@btm.de (ticket and hotel reservations, vacation packages)
Phone service Mon–Fri 8:00 am to 7:00 pm, Sat, Sun 9:00 am to 6:00 pm

Berlin infostores are located at:
Hauptbahnhof, Level 0, northern entrance, daily 8:00 am to 10:00 pm

Brandenburg Gate, April–Oct daily 9:30 am to 6:00 pm, Nov–March daily 10:00 am to 6:00 pm
Alexanderplatz, April–Oct daily 9:30 am to 6:00 pm, Nov–March daily 10:00 am to 6:00 pm
Neues Kranzler Eck, Kurfürstendamm 21, April–Oct Mon–Sat 10:00 am to 8:00 pm, Sun 10:00 am to 6:00 pm, Nov–March daily 10:00 am to 6:00 pm
Berlin Pavillon am Reichstag, Scheidemannstr., April–Oct daily 8:30 am to 8:00 pm, Nov–March daily 10:00 am to 6:00 pm
Europa Center, Budapester Str. 45, April–Oct Mon–Sat 9:00 am to 7:00 pm, Sun 10:00 am to 6:00 pm, Nov–March daily 10:00 am to 6 pm
Further information points can be found at the airports.

Daily newspapers

There are several daily newspapers. The **Berliner Morgenpost** contains extensive coverage of local news.

City magazines

Berlin Programm (monthly) as well as the **TIP** and **Zitty** magazines (biweekly) publish reports about city life, art and cultural events, clubs and parties as well as a detailed event calendar. **Siegessäule** monthly magazine for gays and lesbians is free in bars and many other venues. TIP and Zitty also publish the annual restaurant guide **Berlins Speisekarte** and the bar and club guide **Zitty Spezial Essen Trinken Tanzen**, as well as the shopping guides **Shopping, Lifestyle**, and **Zitty Spezial Shopping**.

Websites

General

www.btm.de – Berlin Tourismus Marketing website
www.berlin.de – Official website of Berlin

Going out

www.berlinatnight.de – Places to go (bars, clubs, restaurants, cafes, beer gardens, beach bars, galleries), hotels, events, theaters, concerts, movies; includes links and information on public transportation
www.clubcommission.de – Current club and party calendar
www.restaurantfuehrer-berlin.de – Addresses of restaurants and bars

Art & culture

www.art-in-berlin.de – Current and permanent exhibitions and museums
www.klassik-in-berlin.de – Internet portal for classical music in Berlin, including current opera and concert schedule
www.smb.spk-berlin.de – Official website of the National Museums in Berlin
www.stadtentwicklung.berlin.de/denkmal – Information on the most significant monuments in Berlin

Sports & recreation

www.berlinerbaederbetriebe.de – Information on all public indoor and outdoor swimming pools, beaches and saunas
www.citysports.de/berlin – Comprehensive list of sports and recreation options

City map

www.berliner-stadtplan.com

Accomodation

www.berlin-tourist-information.de – Hotel booking service of Berlin Tourismus Marketing
www.berlinzimmer.de – Hotels, bed & breakfast, rooms, etc.
www.berliner-hotelzimmer.de – Hotels and bed & breakfast

Events calender

Comprehensive online event schedule published by city magazines and Berliner Morgenpost newspaper.

www.berlinonline.de
www.berlin-programm.de
www.morgenpost.de
www.zitty.de

SIGHTSEEING

City tours

Buses and tramways

Taking the bus or tram is the cheapest way of touring the city. **Bus no. 100** and **bus no. 200**, which run between Bahnhof Zoo and Alexanderplatz, pass some of the main attractions. A **tramway ride** on line **M1** takes you from Bahnhof Friedrichstraße to Prenzlauer Berg, passing the famous Hackesche Höfe and the Scheunenviertel on the way.

Sightseeing buses

There are several companies offering rides on sightseeing buses starting on the corner of Kurfürstendamm and Meinekestraße. A City Circle Tour takes two hours. There are 15 stops where passengers can get off the bus. From April to November bus tours can be combined with a one-hour boat tour on the River Spree. April–Oct 10:00 am to 6:00 pm every 15 min, Nov–March 10:00 am to 5:00 pm every 30 min; 20 €/person, 28 €/person incl. boat tour. For further information contact bus companies:
Berolina Sightseeing, phone +49 (0)30 / 88 56 80 30, www.berolina-berlin.com
Berliner-Bären-Stadtrundfahrt, phone +49 (0)30 / 35 19 52 70, www.bbsberlin.de
Severin & Kühn, phone +49 (0)30 / 8 80 41 90, www.severin-kuehn-berlin.de

Velotaxi

A Velotaxi is an egg-shaped three-wheel bicycle which you can hire for a ride through the city center. These modern rickshaws can be found at Kurfürstendamm, Potsdamer Platz, Tiergarten, and Unter den Linden. 30 min. 7.50 €/person.
Phone: +49 (0)30 / 4 43 19 40.

Trabi "Safari"

A very exotic way of discovering Berlin is in a Trabant, the favorite car of GDR times. After a short technical introduction to the car, which is sometimes sarcastically referred to as "plastic bomber," you can get behind the wheel and for 90 minutes you can enjoy a tour through the city at a speed of 19 mph. You can choose between the Berlin Classic Route and the Wild East Route "safari." If you switch on the radio, you will receive information about Berlin's attractions. Daily 10:00 am to 6:00 pm, starting point at Gendarmenmarkt. 25–35 €/person, www.high-live.de.

Boat tours

From the middle of March to the middle of November, visitors have the opportunity to discover Berlin from a boat on the river. River boat tours take one hour or more. The main stops in the center are at Jannowitzbrücke, Unter den Linden/Schlossbrücke, Berlin Cathedral/Museum Island, Friedrichstraße/ Weidendammer Brücke, Hansabrücke and Schlossbrücke/Charlottenburg. For further information contact the boat companies:

Reederei Riedel, phone +49 (0)30 / 6 93 46 46, www.reederei-riedel.de

Stern- und Kreisschifffahrt, phone +49 (0)30 / 53 63 60-0, www.sternundkreis.de

Reederei Winkler, phone +49 (0)30 / 34 99 59 33, www.reedereiwinkler.de

Sightseeing flights

Airservice Berlin
Phone: +49 (0)30 / 53 21 53 21

Circle above Berlin in a candy bomber, seaplane, or helicopter (from around 86 €/person), or take the Hi-Flyer captive balloon and rise into the air at Checkpoint Charlie (19 €/person).

Guided tours

art:berlin
Heckmann Höfe, Oranienburger Str. 32
Phone: +49 (0)30 / 28 09 63 90
www.artberlin-online.de
In organized tours you get to know Berlin's cultural, artistic and urban landscapes. The tours take you to the Reichstag, the government quarter and embassy buildings, and other destinations; they give you an insight into life in a typical Berlin neighborhood, the art and culture of Berlin, or the worlds of fashion and literature; other tour themes include soccer, movies, hotels or culinary delights.

StattReisen Berlin
Malplaquetstr. 5
Phone: +49 (0)30 / 4 55 30 28
http://stattreisenberlin.de/berlin/
Walks around the city with a focus on history, society and politics which give you an opportunity to take a look behind the curtains.

Stadtverführung
Malmöer Str. 6
Phone: +49 (0)30 / 4 44 09 36
www.stadtverfuehrung.de
A broad variety of guided tours throughout Berlin taking you to historical monuments as well as examples of modern architecture. Tours have historical or contemporary themes.

Viewing the city from above

Television Tower
Panoramastr. 1 a
www.berlinerfernsehturm.de
Observation deck at a height of 666 feet as well as rotating cafe at a height of 679 feet. Daily 10:00 am to midnight, 8 €/person.

Radio tower at the trade fair ground
Berlin-Charlottenburg
Observation deck at a height of 413 feet. Mon 11:00 am to 9:00 pm, Tue–Sun 10:00 am to 11:00 pm, 4 €/person.

Panoramapunkt
Potsdamer Platz 1
www.panoramapunkt.de
Take the fastest elevator in Europe up the Kollhoff

Tower to the observation deck at a height of 328 feet. Daily 11:00 am to 8:00 pm, 3.50 €/person.

TICKETS & DISCOUNTS

Ticket offices

HEKTICKET
www.hekticket.de
Wide range of tickets for concerts, cabaret, theater and other events in Berlin.

HEKTICKET (opposite Bahnhof Zoo train station)
Hardenbergstr. 29d, in the foyer of Deutsche Bank
For advance sales phone +49 (0)30 / 23 09 93 33
For last minute offers phone +49 (0)30 / 2 30 99 30
Fax: +49 (0)30 / 23 09 93 32
Mon–Sat 10:00 am to 8:00 pm, Sun 2:00 pm to 6:00 pm

HEKTICKET (at Alexanderplatz)
Karl-Liebknecht-Str. 12
Phone: +49 (0)30 / 24 31 24 31
Fax: +49 (0)30 / 24 31 24 32
Mon–Sat noon to 8:00 pm

Reductions

Berlin WelcomeCard
Free trips on all public transportation in the specified VBB region (fare regions A,B, and C) as well as a 50% discount on tickets for over 120 different tourist attractions and cultural venues for adults and up to three children under 15. Available online at BTM as well as in the Berlin infostores, numerous hotels, BVG and S-Bahn ticket machines, etc. A ticket for 48 hours costs 16 €, ticket for 72 hours costs 22 €.

SchauLUST-MuseenBERLIN
Admission to over 70 museums and exhibitions for three consecutive days for 15 €, or 7.50 € reduced rate.

GETTING AROUND IN BERLIN

Public transportation

Berliner Verkehrsbetriebe – BVG
Phone: +49 (0)30 / 1 94 49
www.bvg.de
S-Bahn Berlin
Phone: +49 (0)30 / 29 74 33 33
www.s-bahn-berlin.de
Berlin has a very good public transportation network including subways, tramways, S-Bahn trains and buses. There are also night buses and trains to ensure mobility around the clock. Tickets for the fare regions A and B (2.10 €) are valid for all trips within Berlin, short trip tickets (1.20 €) are valid in the city center only. The Berlin WelcomeCard (see above) allows unlimited use of public transportation. The schedules are available for download on the BVG homepage.

Taxi
Phone: +49 (0)30 / 26 10 26, phone: +49 (0)30 / 44 33 22, Phone: +49 (0)8 00 / 2 22 22 55, phone: +49 (0)8 00 / 2 63 00 00

Bicycle rentals

Fahrradstation
Phone: +49 (0)1 80 / 5 10 80 00 (12 ct/Min.)
http://fahrradstation.de
Rent is 10 €/day, location e.g. Friedrichstraße train station (Friedrichstr. 95, entrance at Dorotheenstr. 30)
March–Oct daily 8:00 am to 8:00 pm

Call a Bike

Bicycle rental service of the Deutsche Bahn railway company
For registration phone: +49 (0)7 00 / (0)5 22 55 22 (from 6.2 € ct/Min.)
or register online at: www.callabike-interaktiv.de
Rent is 7 € ct/min. or max. 15 €/day (24 hrs); bicycles are rented via cell phone, payment is by credit card or direct debit.

A bicycle route finder for Berlin (BBBike) is available online at:
http://bbbike.radzeit.de/cgi-bin/bbbike.cgi

EVENTS

International Green Week

International agricultural fair in the middle of January, including samples of international cuisine (www.gruenewoche.de).

The Long Night of Museums

Twice a year, at the end of January and the end of August, Berlin's museums are open to the public for one entire night; this night is usually accompanied by various additional cultural events. (www.lange-nacht-der-museen.de).

Berlin Sixdays

Six day bicycle race, end of January, top sports event in the Velodrom stadium, with accompanying show events (www.sechstagerennen-berlin.de).

Berlin International Film Festival—Berlinale

In early February; attended by many international movie stars; showing top movies (www.berlinale.de).

International Tourism Fair

The most important fair for travel and tourism around the world (www.itb-berlin.de).

berlin biennial

Festival of international contemporary art; begins in March every two years (next in 2010) (www.berlinbiennale.de).

Carnival of Cultures

End of May; colorful procession through the streets of Berlin and celebration in the streets in Kreuzberg with participants from over 80 different cultures (www.karneval-berlin.de).

Christopher Street Day—CSD

End of July; celebration in the streets and gay and lesbian parade (www.csd-berlin.de).

Love Parade

Middle of July; techno music festival, a loud procession through the streets of Berlin (www.loveparade.net).

Internationale Funkausstellung—IFA

Early September; latest developments in the high-tech and consumer electronics sectors (www.ifa-berlin.de).

International Literature Festival Berlin

Middle of September; readings by famous authors and newcomers (www.berlinerfestspiele.de).

Berlin Marathon

End of September (www.berlin-marathon.com).

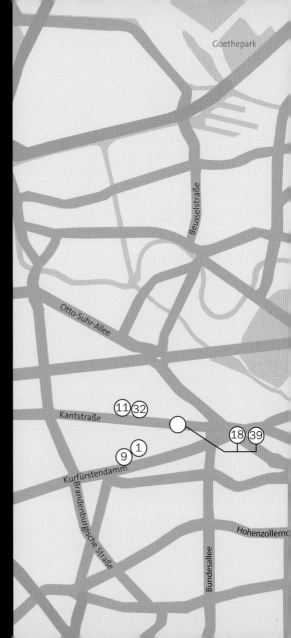

RESTAURANTS & CAFÉS

Adnan

Schlüterstraße 33
10629 Berlin
Charlottenburg
Phone: +49 / 30 / 54 71 05 90

Opening hours: Mon–Sat noon to 1 am
Prices: €€€
Cuisine: Central European
Public transportation: S Savignyplatz
Map: No. 1

Without its charming chef, this would be an Italian restaurant with good food and the noise volume of a Sicilian trattoria. But thanks to Mr. Adnan, a visit to the restaurant that bears his name becomes an experience in itself. From celebrities to just plain folks, you sit side by side with your neighbors and find yourself in easy conversation. Old Berliners, more recent arrivals, and tourists all eat and drink together just like on their last trip to Italy.

Ohne seinen charmanten Chef wäre es ein italienisches Restaurant mit guter Küche und der Lautstärke einer sizilianischen Trattoria. Durch Herrn Adnan wird der Besuch im gleichnamigen Restaurant jedoch zum Erlebnis. Ob Promi oder nicht, man sitzt dicht an dicht und kommt schnell ins Gespräch. Berliner Urgesteine, Zugezogene und Touristen essen und trinken zusammen wie beim letzten Italienurlaub.

Sans son charmant patron, cet endroit ne serait ni plus ni moins qu'un restaurant italien de plus proposant une cuisine honnête et aux décibels d'une trattoria sicilienne. Mais Monsieur Adnan, dans ce restaurant du même nom, se charge de faire de chaque visite une expérience inoubliable. Célébrité ou Monsieur Tout-le-monde, les tables se touchent et on se met à discuter tout naturellement avec ses voisins. Berlinois de souche, nouveaux venus et touristes sont tous rassemblés tels les convives autour d'une grande table comme il en est coutume en Italie.

Sin el encanto personal del jefe de cocina, Adnan sería un buen restaurante italiano con un ruido digno de una trattoria siciliana. La sola presencia del señor Adnan hace de cada visita un auténtico acontecimiento. Los comensales, famosos o no, se apretujan en las mesas y pronto traban conversación, y así los berlineses de pura cepa comparten mesa y comida con los recién llegados y los turistas, como en las vacaciones.

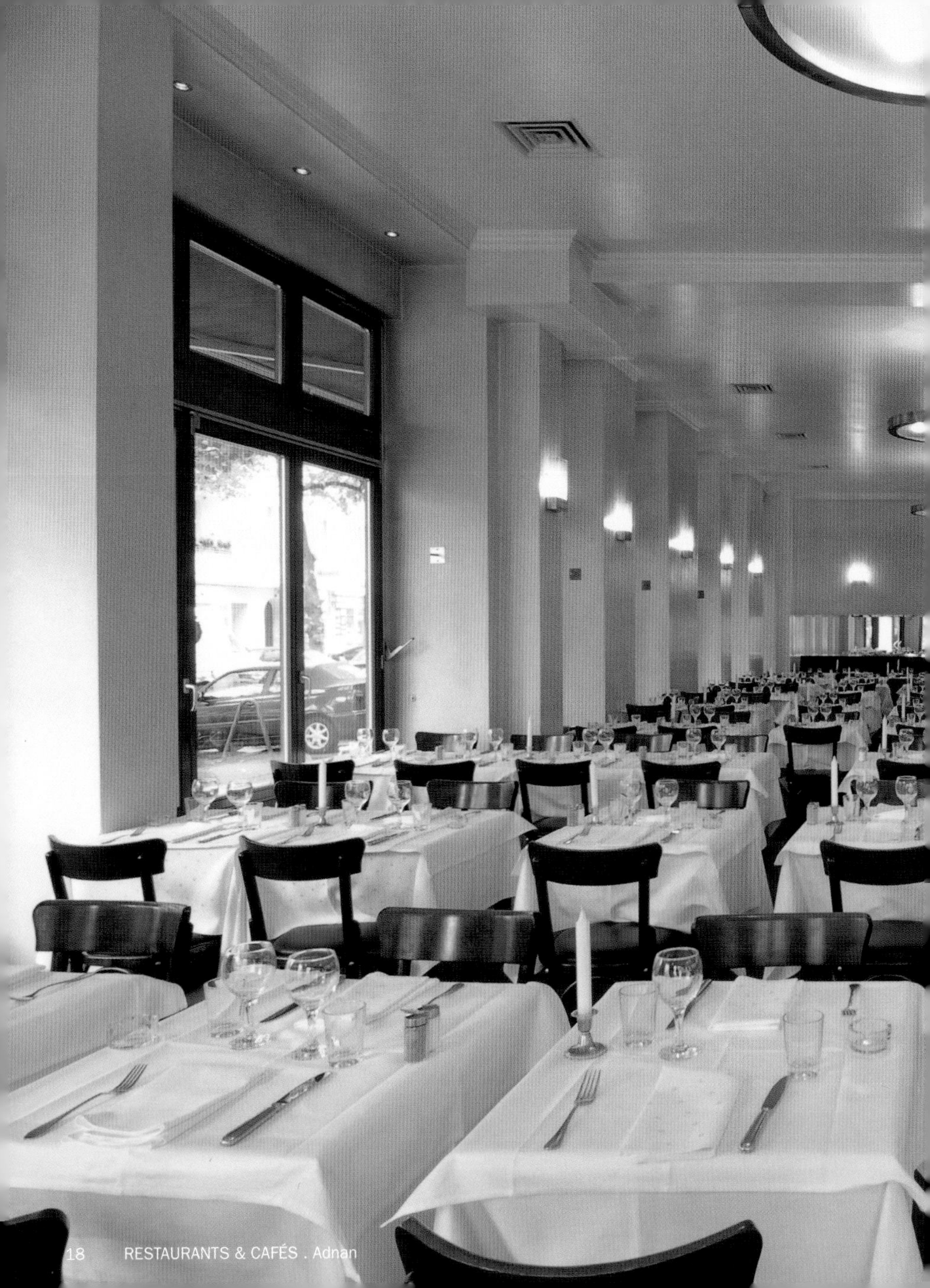

Alpenstueck

Gartenstraße 9
10115 Berlin
Mitte
Phone: +49 / 30 / 21 75 16 46
www.alpenstueck.de

Opening hours: Daily 6 pm to 1 am
Prices: €€
Cuisine: Austrian, Southern German
Public transportation: S Nordbahnhof
Map: No. 2

Tita von Hardenberg's Special Tip
The chefs here don't think much of food combining diets. The high-class cuisine is strictly German and hearty, and the interior design unsurpassed.

True to its name ("a piece of the Alps"), this restaurant brings the charm of snow-covered forests and log cabins to the big city. Both the food and the atmosphere reflect a successful modern urban interpretation of the southern German outlook on life. A simple concrete floor meets a wall of stacked logs. The elegant presentation of Swabian meat-filled pasta brings back memories of vacations spent in the mountains.

Das Restaurant hält was der Name verspricht und bringt das Flair von schneebedeckten Wäldern und Holzhütten in die Großstadt. Sowohl kulinarisch als auch atmosphärisch ist eine modern-urbane Interpretation von süddeutschem Lebensgefühl gelungen. Ein schlichter Gussbetonboden wird mit einer Wand aus aufgeschichteten Holzscheiten kombiniert. Auf dem Teller erinnert die raffiniert angerichtete Maultasche an Urlaube in den Bergen.

Un restaurant au nom révélateur qui tient toutes ses promesses et qui confère à la métropole ce charme si particulier des forêts enneigées et chalets en bois. Une interprétation des plus réussies à la fois moderne et urbaine de l'art de vivre propre à l'Allemagne du Sud tant au niveau de son éventail gastronomique que pour son ambiance. Un mur constitué de bûches repose sur un simple sol en béton coulé. Les « Maultaschen » (raviolis souabes) et leur présentation raffinée ravivent le souvenir heureux des vacances passées à la montagne.

El restaurante hace honor a su nombre y traslada a la ciudad el ambiente de los bosques alpinos y las idílicas cabañas perdidas en la nieve. Tanto en su atmósfera como en su oferta culinaria consigue reinterpretar en clave urbana todo el encanto de la vida en el sur de Alemania. Notable la combinación de un simple suelo de cemento con la pared compuesta de leños apilados. Los exquisitos *maultaschen* que aquí se sirven traen a la memoria las vacaciones en la montaña.

Anna Blume

Kollwitzstraße 83
10435 Berlin
Prenzlauer Berg
Phone: +49 / 30 / 44 04 87 49
www.cafe-anna-blume.de

Opening hours: Daily 8 am to 2 am
Prices: €
Public transportation: U Eberswalder Straße, Senefelderplatz
Map: No. 3

Drawing its name from a poem by Kurt Schwitters and located in a picturesque corner of Prenzlauer Berg, Anna Blume is the number one spot for an extended Sunday brunch or a piece of homemade cake to go with your coffee. Guests of the art deco café enjoy a generously proportioned terrace in summertime. The adjoining flower shop makes bouquets and arrangements that bring to mind paintings by Klimt and Mucha.

Benannt nach einem Gedicht von Kurt Schwitters und in einem malerischen Teil des Prenzlauer Bergs gelegen, ist Anna Blume die erste Adresse für ein ausgiebiges Sonntagsfrühstück oder ein Stück hausgemachten Kuchen zum Kaffee. Das im Art-déco-Stil eingerichtete Café wird im Sommer durch eine großzügige Terrasse erweitert. Der angeschlossene Blumenladen fertigt Gestecke und Dekorationen, die an Bilder von Klimt und Mucha erinnern.

Baptisé ainsi en hommage à un poème de Kurt Schwitters et situé dans un coin pittoresque du quartier de Prenzlauer Berg, l'Anna Blume est devenu le rendez-vous privilégié des amateurs de copieux petits-déjeuners ou de pauses-café et gâteaux faits maison. Le café, dont l'intérieur est aménagé dans le style Art déco, se prolonge en été en une généreuse terrasse. Juste à côté se trouve un fleuriste proposant des compositions et décorations florales qui rappellent les œuvres de Klimt et de Mucha.

Bautizado con el título de un poema de Kurt Schwitter y ubicado en un pintoresco rincón de Prenzlauer Berg, Anna Blume es el mejor local imaginable para disfrutar de un largo desayuno dominical o de un trozo de tarta con el que acompañar el café. El establecimiento, de estilo art déco, cuenta en verano con terraza propia. La floristería contigua prepara ramos y centros de mesa que recuerdan las imágenes de Klimt y Mucha.

Bocca di Bacco

Friedrichstraße 167–168
10117 Berlin
Mitte
Phone: +49 / 30 / 20 67 28 28
www.boccadibacco.de

Opening hours: Mon–Sat noon to midnight, Sun 6 pm to midnight
Prices: €€
Cuisine: Italian with specialities from Tuscany
Public transportation: U Französische Straße
Map: No. 4

Popular for years, this place goes far beyond your standard pizza and noodle dishes. The pasta is hand-made and presented in creative combinations. Chef Loriano Mura also shows inventiveness in the main courses. A high standard of cuisine and modern atmosphere is a popular combination in the capital, so the desirable tables are in correspondingly high demand.

Eine seit Jahren beliebte Adresse jenseits von Pizza und Standardnudeln. Die Pasta ist handgemacht und wird in originellen Kombinationen serviert. Auch bei den Hauptgerichten gibt sich Chefkoch Loriano Mura kreativ. Essen auf hohem Niveau in modernem Ambiente ist eine beliebte Kombination bei den Hauptstädtern und die Nachfrage nach den begehrten Plätzen ist entsprechend groß.

Prisé depuis des années, ce haut lieu de la gastronomie italienne n'a cure des pizzas et pâtes industrielles. La « pasta », faite à la main, est mise à l'honneur dans différentes créations originales. Les plats de résistance sont également relevés d'une pointe de créativité dont seul le chef cuisinier, Loriano Mura, détient le secret. Une cuisine de haut niveau dans un cadre moderne, un subtil mariage en vogue auprès des Berlinois, et la demande est à l'avenant.

Local de enorme éxito y tradición que va más allá de la oferta habitual de pizzas y pasta. Esta última es de fabricación propia y se sirve en originalísimas combinaciones, aunque Loriano Mura, el chef, da rienda suelta a su creatividad también en los segundos. En toda capital se sabe apreciar la combinación de comida de gran nivel y ambiente moderno, de ahí que las mesas del local sean muy codiciadas.

Bonanza Coffee Heroes

Oderberger Straße 35
10435 Berlin
Prenzlauer Berg
Phone: +49 / 178 / 1 44 11 23
www.bonanzacoffee.de

Opening hours: Mon–Fri 9 am to 7 pm, Sat+Sun 10 am to 7 pm
Prices: €
Public transportation: U Eberswalder Straße
Map: No. 5

When a Korean connects the word coffee with art, a Berliner is perplexed; since Coffee Heroes, however, that's a thing of the past. Kiduk and Yumi, members of the international "Third Wave" community dedicated to coffee culture, have brought the Germans' favorite hot beverage to perfection. The Synesso Cyncra coffeemaker, of which there are only three in all Europe, turns finely harmonized bean mixtures into exquisite delicacies.

Wenn ein Koreaner das Wort Kaffee mit Kunst verbindet, wird der Berliner stutzig; seit den Coffee Heroes ist das passé. Bei Kiduk und Yumi, Mitgliedern der internationalen Gemeinschaft „Third Wave", die sich der Kaffeekultur verschrieben hat, wird das beliebteste Heißgetränk der Deutschen zur Vollendung gebracht. Die Synesso Cyncra Kaffeemaschine, von der es europaweit nur drei Exemplare gibt, macht aus edlen Bohnenmischungen feine Köstlichkeiten.

Lorsqu'un Coréen associe le mot « café » à une œuvre d'art, le Berlinois a de quoi être intrigué. Depuis les Coffee Heroes, la stupeur s'est nettement estompée. Chez Kiduk et Yumi, membres du mouvement international Café « troisième vague » dédié à la culture du café, la boisson chaude préférée des Allemands est préparée à la perfection. La machine à café Cyncra de Synesso, dont seuls trois exemplaires existent dans toute l'Europe, transforme mélanges de grains précieux en succulents délices.

Cuando un coreano vincula la palabra "café" con el arte, los berlineses sienten cierta suspicacia, pero desde que existe Coffee Heroes esa desconfianza ha desaparecido. En el local de Kiduk y Yumi, miembros de la comunidad internacional "Third Wave", la bebida caliente favorita de los alemanes alcanza nuevas cotas de perfección. Cuentan con una cafetera Synesso Cyncra, de la que en toda Europa sólo existen tres ejemplares y con la que producen extraordinarias mezclas.

Borchardt

Französische Straße 47
10117 Berlin
Mitte
Phone: +49 / 30 / 81 88 62 62

Opening hours: Daily 11.30 am to open end
Prices: €€€
Cuisine: German, French
Public transportation: U Französische Straße; U, S Friedrichstraße
Map: No. 6

Eva Padberg's Special Tip
Probably the most famous restaurant in Berlin, the food is always top-notch and the atmosphere is great. Magical during the Berlinale—the ultimate in seeing and being seen.

As far back as 1992, Borchardt has been considered "Berlin's dining room"—a locale on everyone's lips where politicians, media personalities, actors, and other celebrities in this metropolis meet for lunch or dinner. Even during the time of the Kaisers, the name Borchardt was a guarantee of quality as a purveyor to the imperial court. The Borchardt catering team continues that tradition down to the present day.

Schon seit 1992 gilt das Borchardt als das „Berliner Esszimmer", ein viel besprochener Ort, wo sich Politiker, Mediengrößen, Schauspieler und andere Persönlichkeiten der Metropole zum Lunch oder Dinner treffen. Der Name Borchardt war schon in wilhelminischer Zeit ein Garant für Qualität, als Hoflieferant für den Kaiser. Diese Tradition setzt das Borchardt Catering Team heute fort.

Le Borchardt est considéré depuis 1992 comme la « salle à manger de Berlin », un lieu dont la réputation n'est plus à faire et où hommes politiques, personnalités médiatiques, acteurs et autres grands noms de la métropole se donnent rendez-vous pour déjeuner ou dîner. Déjà à l'époque wilhelmienne, le nom Borchardt, honoré du titre de fournisseur de la cour impériale, était garant de qualité. De nos jours, l'équipe de restauration Borchardt s'applique à perpétuer cette tradition.

Desde 1992, Borchardt pasa por ser el "comedor" de Berlín, un local muy admirado en el que políticos, actores, periodistas y otros famosos de la ciudad se reúnen para comer y cenar. En tiempos del káiser Guillermo, Borchardt era ya garantía de calidad por su condición de proveedor de la corte. Borchardt Catering Team mantiene viva la tradición en nuestros días.

Café Einstein Stammhaus

Kurfürstenstraße 58
10785 Berlin
Tiergarten
Phone: +49 / 30 / 2 61 50 96
www.cafeeinstein.com

Opening hours: Daily 8 am to 1 pm
Prices: €€€€
Cuisine: Austrian, German
Public transportation: U Nollendorfplatz, Kurfürstenstraße
Map: No. 7

Eva Padberg's Special Tip
You enter the café in a fantastic mansion and you feel like you're in a beautiful, traditional coffee house in the middle of Vienna. Just terrific! A relaxed atmosphere and great food...

The wood paneling and marble tables try to out gleam each other, books are arrayed in glass cases, and waiters in black-and-white uniforms move about serving specialty coffee drinks. For more than thirty years, reading the newspaper over your morning cup of freshly brewed Arabica at Einstein has been an institution. It's not just politicians who appreciate this time-honored café in its 1920s mansion.

Die hölzerne Wandvertäfelung glänzt mit den Marmortischen um die Wette, in Glasvitrinen stehen Bücher, dazwischen servieren Kellner in schwarz-weißer Uniform Kaffeespezialitäten. Seit mehr als 30 Jahren ist der Blick in die Tageszeitung bei der morgendlichen Tasse frisch gebrühtem Arabica im Einstein eine Institution. Nicht nur Politiker schätzen das altehrwürdige Café in der 20er-Jahre-Villa.

Les boiseries murales et les tables en marbre rivalisent de brillance, des livres trônent dans leurs vitrines, un décor à travers lequel des serveurs, de noir et blanc vêtus, vous proposent des spécialités à base de café. Parcourir le journal du matin tout en dégustant son arabica, fraîchement préparé, au café Einstein, une véritable institution depuis plus de 30 ans. Les hommes politiques ne sont pas les seuls à apprécier cette enseigne respectable hébergée dans une villa cossue des années 20.

La madera de las paredes reluce casi tanto como las mesas de mármol, y frente a las vitrinas repletas de libros los camareros uniformados sirven cafés de todo tipo. El vistazo matinal a la prensa en el Einstein frente a una taza de arabica recién hecha tiene en Berlín más de 30 años de tradición. El establecimiento ocupa una venerable mansión de los años veinte y es punto de encuentro habitual de políticos.

Cookies Cream

Behrenstraße, between Westin Grand Hotel and Komische Oper
10178 Berlin
Mitte
Phone: +49 / 30 / 27 49 29 40
www.cookiescream.com

Opening hours: Tue–Sat, 7 pm to open end
Prices: €€
Cuisine: Modern vegetarian cuisine
Public transportation: U Französische Straße; S Unter den Linden
Map: No. 8

Tita von Hardenberg's Special Tip
Guests here start partying while they are dining. Mixed drinks serve as appetizers, while cool interiors and model-perfect staff make for the start of a long night.

Heinz Gindullis, alias Cookie, is among the best-known representatives of the Berlin club scene. His restaurant, reopened in 2007, is located directly above the legendary Cookies Club, whose entrance can be discerned only from the line of people standing in front of it. Chef Stephan Hentschel and his team serve strictly vegetarian dishes to members of the scene and other guests in a lounge atmosphere.

Heinz Gindullis, alias Cookie ist einer der bekanntesten Vertreter der Berliner Clubszene. Das 2007 wiedereröffnete Restaurant befindet sich direkt über dem legendären Cookies Club, dessen Eingang nur durch die Menschenschlange davor auszumachen ist. Chefkoch Stephan Hentschel und sein Team servieren Szenegängern und anderen Gästen puristische vegetarische Gerichte in Lounge-Atmosphäre.

Heinz Gindullis, surnommé Cookie, est une des figures les plus connues de la scène nocturne de Berlin. Le restaurant, qui a rouvert ses portes en 2007, se trouve juste au-dessus du légendaire club Cookies, dont il est impossible de manquer l'entrée en raison de l'impressionnante file d'attente. Le chef cuisinier Stephan Hentschel et son équipe proposent à une foule bigarrée (habitués branchés comme grand public) des plats végétariens pour le plus grand plaisir des véritables puristes dans un sobre décor de salon.

Heinz Gindullis, alias Cookie, es uno de los más conocidos empresarios de la noche berlinesa. El restaurante, reabierto en 2007, se encuentra directamente frente al legendario Cookies Club, cuya entrada apenas puede entreverse tras las largas colas que frente a ella se forman. El chef Stephan Hentschel y su equipo presentan ante sus comensales nocturnos platos vegetarianos puristas en una atmósfera elegante y relajada.

Enoiteca Il Calice

Walter-Benjamin-Platz 4
10629 Berlin
Charlottenburg
Phone: +49 / 30 / 3 24 23 08
www.enoiteca-il-calice.de

Opening hours: Mon–Sat noon to 2 am, Sun 5 pm to 2 am
Prices: €€€
Cuisine: Italian
Public transportation: U Adenauerplatz; S Savignyplatz
Map: No. 9

Located on the "piazza" designed by star architect Hans Kollhoff, Enoiteca offers anything a gourmet's heart could desire. Enjoy outstanding antipasti, dolci, and a selection of hot dishes over a glass of any of the seven hundred or so wines on offer. Il Calice embodies the perfection of this tried-and-true format. In the summer, guests can also dine on the elegant terrace.

An der von Stararchitekt Hans Kollhoff gestalteten „Piazza" gelegen, bietet die Enoiteca alles, was das Gourmetherz begehrt. Bei einem Glas der rund 700 angebotenen Weinsorten kann man hervorragende Antipasti, Dolci und eine Auswahl an warmen Speisen genießen. Dieses bewährte Konzept beherrscht das Il Calice bis zur Vollendung. Im Sommer können die Gäste außerdem stilvoll auf der Terrasse speisen.

Aux bords de la « Piazza » conçue par l'architecte de renom Hans Kollhoff, le restaurant Enoiteca offre tout ce dont les fins gourmets rêvent. Antipasti (entrées), dolci (desserts) ainsi qu'une sélection de plats chauds peuvent être dégustés autour d'un verre de l'une des quelque 700 sortes de vin proposées. Le Il Calice porte ce concept éprouvé à son paroxysme. En été, la clientèle peut également se restaurer en terrasse. La grande classe !

Situada en una piazza concebida por el célebre arquitecto Hans Kollhoff, la Enoiteca ofrece todo cuando un gourmet puede desear. Antipasti, dolci y una amplia selección de platos complementan el disfrute de alguno de los 700 vinos que tienen en oferta, un planteamiento clásico y sin embargo efectivo que en Il Calice han sabido llevar hasta la perfección. En verano, los comensales pueden disfrutar de su comida en la terraza.

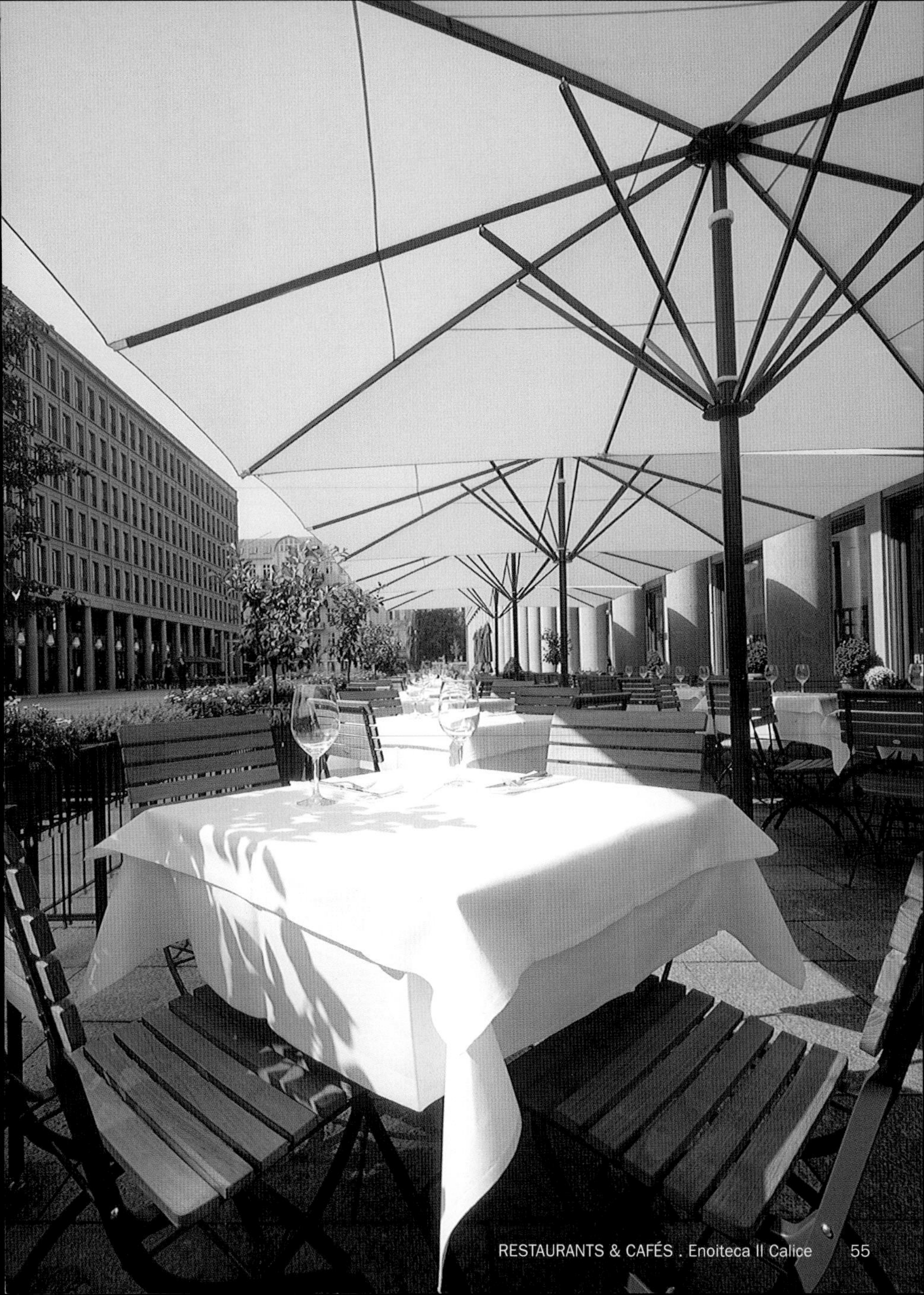

Grill Royal

Friedrichstraße 105b
10117 Berlin
Mitte
Phone: +49 / 30 / 28 87 92 88
www.grillroyal.com

Opening hours: Daily 6 pm to open end
Prices: €€€€
Cuisine: Precious steakhouse
Public transportation: U Oranienburger Tor; S Friedrichstraße
Map: No. 10

Tita von Hardenberg's Special Tip
The smoking room is so inviting that even a non-smoker would like to hang out there. Especially since that's where the real party happens.

Boris Radczun has put out a challenge to Berlin's dusty corner pubs and illegal clubs, restoring some of the capital's old polish. With Grill Royal he has created a place where protagonists from Berlin's up-and-coming art world eat their steak and sip their champagne alongside filmmakers and politicians. Be sure to make a reservation if you want to be part of the scene.

Boris Radczun hat staubigen Berliner Eckkneipen und illegalen Clubs den Kampf angesagt und ein Stück vom alten Glanz der Hauptstadt zurückgeholt. Mit Grill Royal hat er einen Ort geschaffen, an dem die Protagonisten der aufstrebenden Berliner Kunstszene zusammen mit Filmemachern und Politikern ihr Steak essen und an ihrem Champagner nippen. Wer an diesem Schauspiel teilhaben möchte, sollte auf jeden Fall reservieren.

Boris Radczun a déclaré la guerre aux vétustes troquets berlinois et night-clubs illégaux pour redonner à la capitale un peu de sa splendeur d'antan. Le Grill Royal lui a permis de créer un lieu dans lequel les protagonistes de la scène artistique en pleine ascension de Berlin ainsi que cinéastes et hommes politiques se retrouvent pour manger leur steak et siroter leur champagne. Pour assister à ce spectacle, il est vivement recommandé de réserver à l'avance.

Boris Radczun ha declarado la guerra a los vetustos tugurios y los clubs ilegales de Berlín y ha sabido recuperar parte del glamour de la capital. Con Grill Royal ha conseguido crear un local al que acuden cineastas, políticos y los principales protagonistas de la efervescente vida artística de la capital para probar la carne y el champán. Si quiere unirse a ellos, es muy recomendable que reserve mesa con antelación.

Kuchi

Kantstraße 30
10623 Berlin
Charlottenburg
Phone: +49 / 30 / 31 50 78 15
www.kuchi.de

Opening hours: Daily noon to midnight
Prices: €€€
Cuisine: South Eastern Asian, specialising in sushi
Public transportation: S Savignyplatz
Map: No. 11

Eva Padberg's Special Tip
The place for classic and offbeat sushi creations. Whatever you order, it's all yummy and the atmosphere is youthful and modern.

Since 1999, Kuchi has been a favorite address for lovers of maki, nigiri, and the like. A neo-Japanese atmosphere is the setting for enjoying classic specialties and also some innovative creations, as well as hot dishes. The crowd is young and beautiful, and it's not unusual for it to include film and television celebrities.

Seit 1999 ist das Kuchi eine Topadresse für Liebhaber von Maki, Nigiri und sämtlichen Verwandten. In neojapanischem Ambiente genießt man neben den Klassikern auch einige innovative Kreationen sowie warme Gerichte. Das Publikum ist jung, attraktiv und nicht selten ist ein bekanntes Gesicht aus Film und Fernsehen dabei.

Depuis 1999, le Kuchi est le restaurant par excellence des amateurs de makis, nigiris et autres délices du Soleil levant. L'ambiance néo-japonaise invite à la dégustation à la fois de grands classiques, d'une cuisine créative et novatrice ainsi que de plats chauds. Parmi la clientèle, jeune et séduisante, il n'est pas rare de croiser un visage connu du petit et grand écran.

Kuchi es desde 1999 local indispensable para los amantes del aki, el nigiri y otras especialidades niponas. Ante el visitante se abre un espacio de estilo neojaponés en el que además de la selección habitual de platos encontrará también innovadores creaciones y platos calientes. La clientela es joven y atractiva, y a menudo es posible reconocer algún rostro conocido del cine y la televisión.

MÁ Restaurant

Behrenstraße 72
10117 Berlin
Mitte
Phone: +49 / 30 / 3 01 11 73 33
www.ma-restaurants.de

Opening hours: Tue–Sat 7 pm to 11 pm
Prices: €€€€
Cuisine: Chinese cuisine in combination with regional products
Public transportation: U, S Brandenburger Tor
Map: No. 12

Tim Raue's latest restaurant concept on the southern side of Hotel Adlon—consisting of MÁ-Tim Raue, uma, and the Shochu Bar—sets a new culinary standard in Berlin. The cuisine shows Chinese and Japanese influence. Anne Marie Jagdfeld completed the Asian-inspired interior with costly fabrics and art from the Far East.

Tim Raues neues Restaurantkonzept auf der Südseite des Hotel Adlon, bestehend aus dem MÁ-Tim Raue und uma sowie der Shochu Bar, setzt neue gastronomische Maßstäbe in Berlin. Die Küche ist chinesisch und japanisch beeinflusst. Das asiatisch inspirierte Interieur komplettierte Anne Marie Jagdfeld mit edlen Stoffen und fernöstlicher Kunst.

Le nouveau concept de restaurant développé par Tim Raue dans la partie sud de l'hôtel Adlon, regroupant le MÁ-Tim Raue, l'uma ainsi que le Shochu Bar, définit à Berlin de nouveaux standards « gastronomiques ». Une cuisine aux influences à la fois chinoises et japonaises. Un design intérieur de style asiatique agrémenté par les soins d'Anne Marie Jagdfeld d'étoffes précieuses et d'œuvres d'art d'Extrême-Orient.

El novedoso concepto de restauración que Tim Raue ha instalado al socaire del hotel Adlon marca un antes y un después en el panorama gastronómico de Berlín. Compuesto por tres locales (MÁ-Tim Raue, uma y el bar Shochu), ofrece platos de inspiración china y japonesa. Anne Maria Jagdfeld es la responsable del diseño interior, de aires asiáticos subrayados por el uso de las mejores telas y obras de arte orientales.

Spindler & Klatt

Köpenicker Straße 16/17
10997 Berlin
Kreuzberg
Phone: +49 / 30 / 3 19 88 18 60
www.spindlerklatt.com

Opening hours: June–Sept daily 8 pm to open end, Oct–May Thu–Sat 8 pm to open end
Prices: €€€
Cuisine: Panasian
Public transportation: U Schlesisches Tor
Map: No. 13

An old factory hall was converted into an impressive dinner club using mainly mobile furnishings consisting of bar elements and box-section beds combined with extensive light and sound engineering. In 2006 it received the Fizzz Award. Dining is outside with a one-of-a-kind view of the River Spree. Cuisine and atmosphere are Asian-inspired.

Eine alte Fabrikhalle wurde mithilfe einer größtenteils mobilen Einrichtung aus Bar-Elementen und Kastenbetten sowie umfangreicher Licht- und Soundtechnik zu einem beeindruckenden Clubrestaurant umgestaltet. Im Jahre 2006 erhielt es dafür den Fizzz Award. Diniert wird im Außenbereich mit einzigartigem Blick auf die Spree. Küche und Ambiente sind asiatisch inspiriert.

Rénovée à l'aide d'un équipement principalement mobile constitué d'éléments de bar et de lits bateaux, cette ancienne usine, disposant d'un important matériel d'éclairage et de sonorisation, abrite désormais un incroyable restaurant club. En 2006, le prix « Fizzz Award » lui a même été décerné. Espace extérieur pour dîner en plein air, avec vue imprenable sur la Spree. Cuisine et ambiance agrémentées de notes asiatiques.

La antigua nave industrial se ha convertido en un espectacular bar-restaurante gracias a un novedoso concepto interiorista de piezas móviles y un acertado uso de la iluminación y los sistemas de sonido. El diseño del local mereció en 2006 el premio Fizzz. Las comidas se sirven en un espacio exterior con vistas únicas sobre el Spree. La cocina y el ambiente son de inspiración asiática.

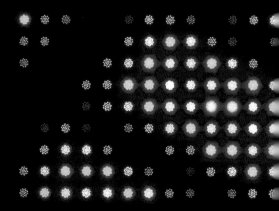

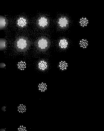

CLUBS,
LOUNGES &
BARS

103 Bar

Kastanienallee 49
10119 Berlin
Prenzlauer Berg
Phone: +49 / 30 / 44 34 11 03
www.agentur103.de

Opening hours: Daily 9 am to open end
Prices: €€
Public transportation: U Eberswalder Straße, Rosenthaler Platz; Tram Zionskirchplatz
Map: No. 14

Don't bother looking for advertising or helpful signs on the exterior. This corner bar on Kastanienallee is a popular venue for the young Berlin scene. Outside seating announces itself in gaudy '70s-style orange, while the inside is dominated by a retro-look lounge atmosphere. In addition to the bar, Agentur 103 offers an Asian snack counter, guesthouse, and an art and performance studio.

Nach Außenwerbung oder Hinweisschildern sucht man vergeblich. Die Eckbar an der Kastanienallee ist ein beliebter Treffpunkt für die junge Berliner Szene. Die Außenbestuhlung präsentiert sich in knalligem 70er-Jahre-Orange, innen herrscht Loungeatmosphäre im Retrodesign. Die Agentur 103 unterhält neben der Bar einen Asia-Imbiss, ein Gästehaus sowie ein Studio für Kunst und Performance.

Pas la peine de chercher la moindre forme d'écriteau ni de publicité extérieure. Le bar à l'angle de la Kastanienallee est devenu l'un des lieux de rendez-vous privilégiés des jeunes Berlinois. Une terrasse parsemée de chaises couleur orange criard des années 70, tandis qu'à l'intérieur règne une ambiance de salon au design rétro. Outre le bar, l'agence 103 dirige également un snack asiatique, une maison d'hôtes ainsi qu'un atelier Art et Performance.

No se esfuerce en buscar carteles anunciadores o reclamo publicitario alguno. El *Eckbar* de Kastanienallee es un popular punto de encuentro de la noche berlinesa. Las sillas del exterior atraen de inmediato la atención por su color chillón naranja años setenta, mientras que la atmósfera interior se caracteriza por un diseño retro de detalles más discretos. La empresa 103 dirige, además del bar, un restaurante asiático de comidas rápidas, un hotel y un escenario de artes y espectáculos.

Bar Tausend

Schiffbauerdamm 11
10117 Berlin
Mitte
Phone: +49 / 30 / 27 58 20 70
www.tausendberlin.com

Opening hours: Tue–Sat 9 pm to open end
Prices: €€€
Public transportation: U, S Friedrichstraße
Map: No. 15

Tita von Hardenberg's Special Tip
This is definitely the city's most attractive bar with the greatest likelihood of getting drunk. Since they started serving delicious fusion cuisine in the Backroom Cantina, there's no longer a reason to leave.

Don't look for a neon advertisement or informative sign to direct you to the entrance of one of the hottest bars in all of Berlin: an inconspicuous iron door with a bell is all you'll find. Once you're inside, you can drink your beverage among a colorful mixture from Berlin's hip scene and a celebrity or two. Bar Tausend is the very definition of a bar.

Keine Leuchtreklame, kein Hinweisschild, nur eine unscheinbare Eisentür mit Klingel bietet den Eingang zu einer der angesagtesten Bars von ganz Berlin. Ist man erstmal drin, kann man seinen Drink zwischen einer bunten Mischung Berliner Szene und dem ein oder anderen prominenten Gesicht zu sich nehmen. Die Bar Tausend ist schlicht der Inbegriff einer Bar.

Aucune enseigne lumineuse, aucun panneau. Seule une porte anodine en fer avec une sonnette fait office d'entrée de l'un des bars les plus branchés du tout Berlin. Une fois à l'intérieur, il ne reste plus qu'à prendre un verre dans un monde où se côtoient allégrement scène berlinoise et célébrités. Le Bar Tausend est tout bonnement l'incarnation même d'un bar.

Ni carteles luminosos ni placas en la entrada: una anodina puerta de hierro y un simple timbre guardan la entrada de uno de los bares más populares de la ciudad. Una vez dentro, el visitante se encontrará en pleno centro de la noche berlinesa, y quizá reconozca alguna que otra cara famosa. El Bar Tausend es, simplemente, un bar en estado puro.

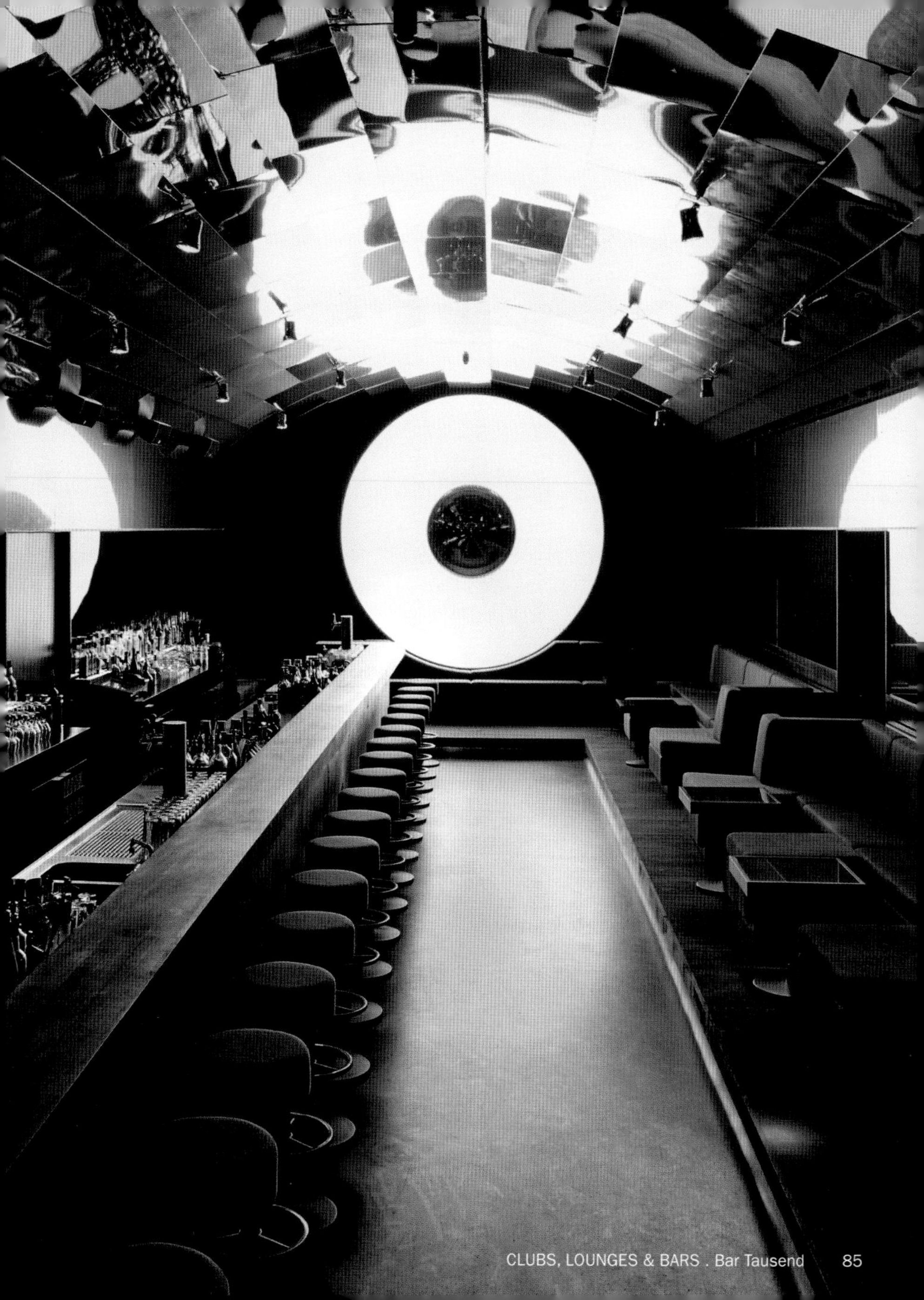

Green Door

Winterfeldtstraße 50
10781 Berlin
Schöneberg
Phone: +49 / 30 / 2 15 25 15
www.greendoor.de

Opening hours: Son–Thu 8 pm to 3 am, Fri–Sat 6 pm to 4 am
Prices: €€
Public transportation: U Nollendorfplatz
Map: No. 16

Tita von Hardenberg's Special Tip
You could find Marilyn Manson sitting at the bar here without anyone being overly impressed. A Berlin classic—the atmosphere is relaxed and the cocktails are skillfully mixed.

After you pass through the door (yes, it's green), what you see is half English country house and half modern bar. Fritz Müller-Scherz—screenwriter, actor, and multipurpose talent—has assembled a bar team that is without equal in the capital. For years, mai tais and other cocktails of exemplary quality have been mixed under the constant supervision of Moritz the Light-Up Dog, who stands watch over the bar.

Wer durch die grüne Tür tritt, findet sich in einer Mischung aus englischem Landhaus und moderner Bar wieder. Fritz Müller-Scherz, Drehbuchautor, Schauspieler und Allroundtalent hat ein Barteam zusammengestellt, das in der Hauptstadt seinesgleichen sucht. Mai Tai & Co. werden seit Jahren in vorbildlicher Qualität gemixt, stets beäugt von Leuchthund Moritz, der über der Theke wacht.

Une porte verte derrière laquelle le charme authentique des cottages anglais et un bar moderne sont subtilement conjugués. Fritz Müller-Scherz, scénariste, acteur et homme aux talents multiples, a mis sur pied une équipe exceptionnelle n'ayant point d'égal dans toute la ville. Depuis des années, le secret des cocktails Mai Tai & Co. réside dans la qualité exemplaire de leur préparation, sous la garde de Moritz, le chien lumineux sur le comptoir.

Quienes cruzan la puerta verde encuentran una mezcla de residencia campestre británica y moderno bar. Fritz Müller-Scherz, guionista, actor y personaje multifacético, ha reunido en él a un equipo incomparable. Desde hace años se sirven aquí cócteles de factura impecable (mai tais y muchos otros), siempre bajo la atenta mirada de Moritz, el perro lámpara que vela sobre la barra.

Solar

Stresemannstraße 76
10963 Berlin
Kreuzberg
Phone: +49 / 163 / 7 65 27 00
www.solarberlin.com

Opening hours: Mon–Thu noon to 2 am, Fri noon to 4 am, Sat 6 pm to 4 am, Sun 6 pm to 2 am
Prices: €€
Public transportation: S Anhalter Bahnhof
Map: No. 17

Assuming the bouncer lets you in, you take a glassed-in exterior elevator to the eighteenth floor of a '70s high-rise. From the elegant lounge at the top, you can enjoy a panoramic view that was once appreciated by the CIA, which kept a listening post here. There is music from the DJ and occasionally a live performance to go with your cocktail and the view. The next floor down houses the retro-style companion restaurant.

Gewährt der Türsteher Einlass, fährt man mit einem gläsernen Außenlift in den 17. Stock eines 70er-Jahre Hochhauses. Oben angekommen, genießt man in der edel gestalteten Lounge einen Panoramablick, den auch die CIA, die hier einen Horchposten unterhielt, schon zu schätzen wusste. Zu Cocktails und Aussicht gibt es Musik vom DJ mit gelegentlichen Live-Einlagen. Im Stockwerk darunter befindet sich das zugehörige Restaurant im Retro-Look.

Une fois la permission d'entrer accordée par le videur, un ascenseur extérieur en verre vous conduit au 17ème étage d'une tour des années 70. Arrivé à destination, vous pouvez profiter depuis le salon au design épuré d'une vue imprenable que même la CIA appréciait déjà à sa juste valeur, ayant par le passé installé un poste d'écoute en ces lieux. Au programme : cocktails, panorama et savoir-faire du DJ ainsi que prestations ponctuelles en live. À l'étage du dessous vous attend son restaurant ambiance rétro.

Tras sortear a los porteros, el visitante asciende en un ascensor exterior vidriado hasta la planta 17 de un bloque de pisos construido en los años setenta. Una vez arriba, el elegantísimo local ofrece espectaculares vistas panorámicas sobre la ciudad: la mismísima CIA mantuvo aquí un puesto de vigilancia. Los cócteles se ven aderezados por la música de un DJ y, en ocasiones, por actuaciones en directo. Un piso más abajo se encuentra el restaurante de los mismos propietarios, decorado en estilo retro.

Vienna Bar

Kantstraße 152
10623 Berlin
Charlottenburg
Phone: +49 / 30 / 31 01 50 90
www.vienna-bar.de

Opening hours: Daily from 5 pm
Prices: €€€
Cuisine: Regional kitchen with Austrian influences
Public transportation: U Uhlandstrasse, Kurfürstendamm; U, S Zoologischer Garten,
S Savignyplatz
Map: No. 18

The west of Berlin is richer by one hot venue. In the location of the former "Bar du Paris Bar," restaurant magnate Josef Laggner has opened a bar adorned with the same unmistakable red neon lettering, albeit with a new name. The remodeled furnishings are still reminiscent of a casual Parisian eatery. While the emphasis is on the drinks, the menu also offers a wide range of choices: from oysters to Wiener Schnitzel to the city's most expensive curried bratwurst.

Der Berliner Westen ist um einen In-Treffpunkt reicher. In den ehemaligen Räumen der „Bar du Paris Bar" hat Großgastronom Josef Laggner eine Bar eröffnet, die die gleiche unverkennbare rote Leuchtschrift ihrer Vorgängerin ziert, allerdings mit neuem Namen. Die renovierte Einrichtung erinnert weiterhin an Pariser Brasserien. Der Fokus liegt zwar auf den Getränken, aber auch die Speisekarte bietet ein breites Angebot: von Austern über Wiener Schnitzel bis hin zur teuersten Currywurst der Stadt.

L'Ouest de Berlin abrite un lieu de rendez-vous branché de plus. Dans les locaux de l'ancien « Bar du Paris Bar », le célèbre restaurateur Josef Laggner a conservé l'enseigne prestigieuse et lumineuse en lettres rouges de son prédécesseur tout en changeant de nom. L'intérieur rénové a quand même gardé les allures de brasserie parisienne. Bien que les boissons soient mises en vedette, un large éventail gastronomique est également proposé, allant des huîtres à la saucisse au curry la plus chère de la ville en passant par l'escalope de veau panée.

Berlín Oeste cuenta desde ahora con otro punto de encuentro indispensable. El restaurador Josef Laggner ha abierto un bar en el antiguo local del Bar du Paris Bar y ha conservado el inconfundible diseño del cartel luminoso de su predecesor, cambiando, eso sí, el nombre. El renovado espacio evoca en parte una brasserie parisina. El alma del negocio son las bebidas, es cierto, pero la carta es bastante extensa, y abarca desde ostras y filetes empanados hasta la más cara salchicha al curry de la ciudad.

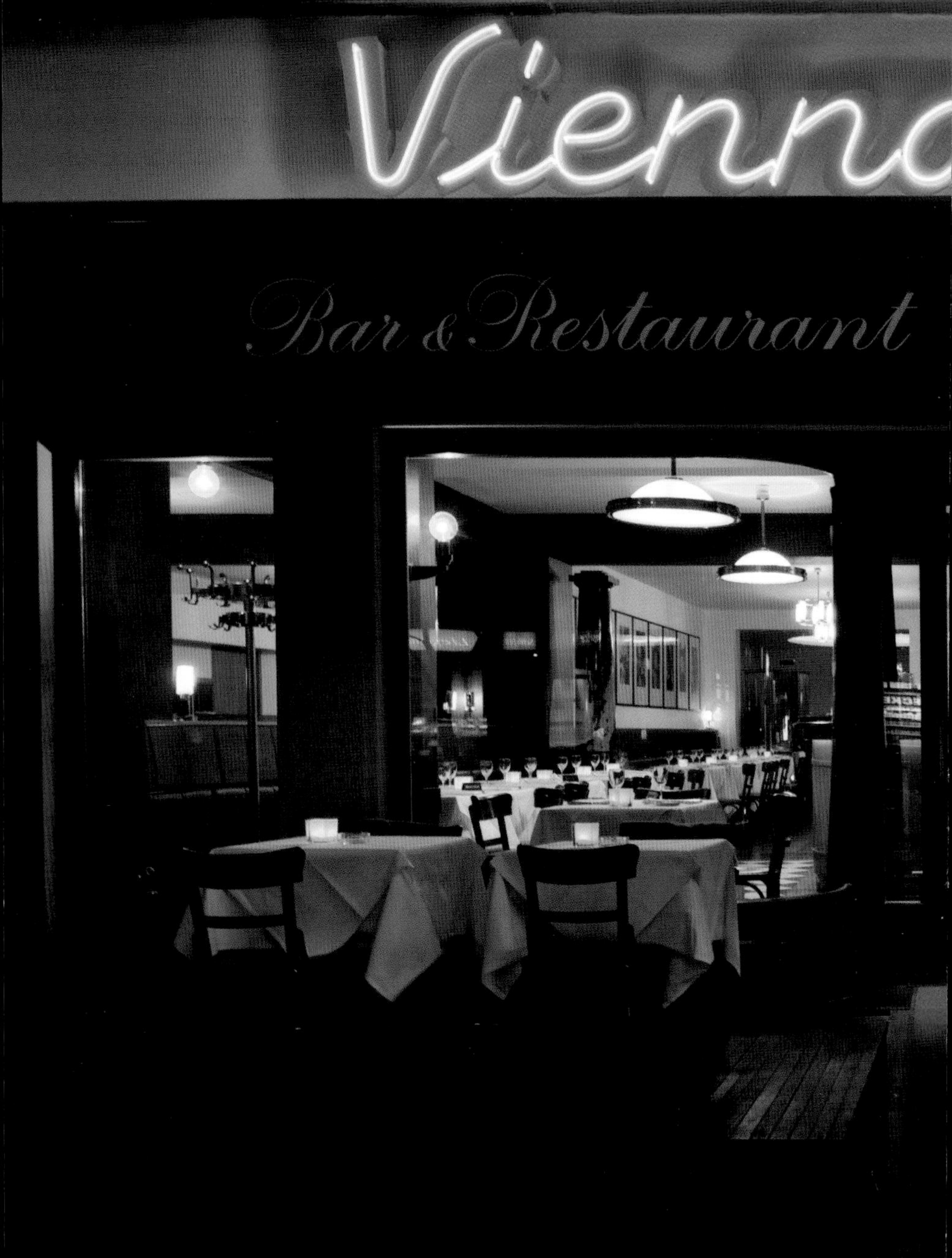
Vienna
Bar & Restaurant

Weekend

Alexanderstraße 7
10178 Berlin
Mitte
Phone: +49 / 30 / 24 63 16 76
www.week-end-berlin.de

Opening hours: Thu, Fri+Sat 11 pm to open end
Prices: €€
Public transportation: U, S Alexanderplatz
Map: No. 19

Eva Padberg's Special Tip
A great club with a view of Alexanderplatz and a huge rooftop deck that draws all the night owls in summer.

An office building during the day, at night its elevator stops only on the thirteenth floor, which the young architectural firm of ROBERTNEUN has transformed into one of the city's most popular nightclubs. In summertime, partiers gather on the roof deck and collectively enjoy the panoramic view of Berlin after dark.

Tagsüber ein Bürogebäude, hält der Aufzug spät abends nur noch im 12. Stock, den das junge Architekturbüro ROBERTNEUN, zu einem der beliebtesten Nachtclubs der Stadt gestaltet hat. Im Sommer versammeln sich die Feiernden auf der Dachterrasse und genießen kollektiv den Panoramablick über das nächtliche Berlin.

Le jour, un banal immeuble de bureaux, dont l'ascenseur dessert dans la soirée seulement le 12ème étage, aménagé par ROBERTNEUN, cabinet de jeunes architectes, en l'une des boîtes de nuit les plus prisées de la ville. En été, les noctambules se donnent rendez-vous sur la terrasse du toit pour apprécier ensemble la vue imprenable sur Berlin *by night*.

De día edificio de oficinas, al caer la noche el ascensor se detiene sólo en el piso 12, acondicionado por el joven despacho de arquitectos ROBERTNEUN para convertirlo en uno de los clubs nocturnos con mayor atractivo de toda la ciudad. En verano, la clientela se agolpa en la azotea para disfrutar de la vista panorámica sobre la noche de Berlín.

SHOPS

4010 – Der Telekom Shop in Mitte

Alte Schönhauser Straße 31
10119 Berlin
Mitte
Phone: +49 / 30 / 24 04 86 34
www.4010.com

Opening hours: Mon–Sat 11 am to 8 pm
Products: T-Mobile, T-Home services
Public transportation: U Weinmeisterstraße; S Hackescher Markt
Map: No. 20

In a creative environment of galleries, agencies, design studios, coffee bars, clubs, and fashion stores, 4010 sees itself as a next-generation telecommunication store. This includes a relaxed atmosphere with a tea bar, lounge, and free Wi-Fi—and also events like readings and concerts. The Concept Room provides space for exhibits and temporary shops, and the Gallery Wall is designed by different artists in succession.

Im kreativen Umfeld von Galerien, Agenturen, Designstudios, Coffee Bars, Clubs und Fashionstores versteht sich der 4010 als Telekommunikationsstore der nächsten Generation. Dazu gehören eine entspannte Atmosphäre mit Teebar, Lounge und kostenlosem Hotspot, aber auch Events wie Lesungen oder Konzerte. Der Concept Room bietet Raum für Ausstellungen und temporäre Shops und die Gallery Wall wird von Künstlern im Wechsel gestaltet.

Dans l'environnement résolument créatif des galeries, agences, studios, cafés, clubs et magasins de mode, le 4010 se définit comme magasin de télécommunication futuriste. Ici, il y a de quoi se sentir à l'aise. Bar à thé, lounge et point d'accès wifi gratuit, il est aussi consacré à l'évènementiel, avec des lectures et des concerts. De son côté, le Concept Room peut accueillir des expositions ainsi que des boutiques temporaires tandis que le Gallery Wall change de look sous l'impulsion des artistes qui y passent.

En el entorno creativo de galerías, agencias, estudios de diseño, cafés, clubs y tiendas de moda, 4010 se define a sí mismo como tienda de telecomunicaciones de la próxima generación. A ello contribuye un ambiente relajado, con bar de tés, lounge y conexión WiFi gratuita, pero también numerosos acontecimientos, como conciertos y presentaciones. El Concept Room ofrece espacio a exposiciones y tiendas de temporadas; una sucesión de artistas rediseña a intervalos la Gallery Wall.

berlinomat

Frankfurter Allee 89
10247 Berlin
Friedrichshain
Phone: +49 / 30 / 42 08 14 45
www.berlinomat.com

Opening hours: Mon–Sat 11 am to 8 pm
Products: Fashion, furniture, jewelry
Public transportation: U Samariterstraße; U, S Frankfurter Allee
Map: No. 21

Here you'll find almost 5,000 square feet of fashions, accessories, and other products exclusively by Berlin designers. In recent years the capital has produced countless creative minds, and this shop in the Friedrichshain district shows a broad spectrum of their art, from the cement television tower to collections by up-and-coming fashion designers. If you want to take home a piece of young Berlin, you should definitely check it out.

Auf 450 m² findet man Mode, Accessoires und andere Produkte, die ausschließlich von Berliner Designern stammen. Die Hauptstadt hat in den letzten Jahren unzählige kreative Köpfe hervorgebracht und der Laden in Friedrichshain zeigt ein breites Spektrum ihrer Kunst, vom Betonfernsehturm bis hin zu Kollektionen aufstrebender Modedesigner. Wer ein Stück junges Berlin mit in die Heimat nehmen möchte, sollte hier vorbeischauen.

Répartis sur 450 m², articles de mode, accessoires et autres produits conçus exclusivement par des designers berlinois. Ces dernières années, la capitale a vu naître d'innombrables esprits créatifs. Et le magasin dans le quartier de Friedrichshain propose un large éventail de leur art, allant de la tour de télévision en béton aux collections d'étoiles montantes de la mode. L'une des meilleures adresses pour ramener chez soi un souvenir du Berlin branché.

450 m² de moda, accesorios y otros muchos productos creados exclusivamente por diseñadores berlineses. La capital ha atraído en años recientes a incontables creadores, y el establecimiento de Friedrichshain muestra un amplio abanico de ideas, desde la torre de televisión en cemento hasta las colecciones de novísimos diseñadores. Obligatorio pasar por allí para quienes deseen llevarse a casa un pedazo del Berlín joven.

blush Dessous

Rosa-Luxemburg-Straße 22
10178 Berlin
Mitte
Phone: +49 / 30 / 28 09 35 80
www.blush-berlin.com

Opening hours: Mon–Fri noon to 8 pm, Sat noon to 7 pm
Products: Dessous, nightwear, sleeping masks, tights (nylons)
Public transportation: U Rosa-Luxemburg-Platz; U, S Alexanderplatz
Map: No. 22

Ladies familiar with Victoria's Secret and Agent Provocateur can't pass up lingerie from Blush. The award-winning concept store specializes in undergarments for women, and now also for men. There is an in-house undergarment label in addition to international makers. Once the perfect piece is found, it can be immediately presented on the "jet bed" in the shop.

Damen, denen Victoria's Secret und Agent Provocateur ein Begriff sind, werden an den Dessous von Blush nicht vorbei kommen. Der preisgekrönte Concept Store hat sich auf das „Darunter" für die Frau und mittlerweile auch für den Mann spezialisiert. Neben internationalen Herstellern gibt es ein hauseigenes Wäschelabel. Ist das perfekte Modell gefunden, kann es gleich auf dem Jet-Bett im Laden präsentiert werden.

Les dames, qui connaissent les noms Victoria's Secret et Agent Provocateur, se doivent de venir apprécier en personne la collection de lingerie de Blush. Le concept store primé s'est spécialisé dans les dessous pour femmes et depuis quelques temps également pour hommes. Outre les produits de stylistes de renommée internationale, la boutique commercialise aussi sa propre marque de sous-vêtements. Une fois le modèle de ses rêves trouvé, il ne reste plus qu'à le passer dans une ambiance intime, « jet-lit » des années 80 trônant au milieu de la boutique.

Quienes estén familiarizadas con marcas como Victoria's Secret y Agent Provocateur no pasarán de largo ante el escaparate de Blush. El galardonado concept store se ha especializado en lencería femenina y, más recientemente en ropa interior masculina. Cuenta además con una línea propia de complementa la extensa oferta de marcas internacionales. Una vez encontrado el modelo perfecto, la casa ofrece la posibilidad de presentarlo sobre una cama escaparate.

bob – boxoffberlin

Zimmerstraße 11
10969 Berlin
Kreuzberg
Phone: +49 / 30 / 44 70 15 55
www.boxoffberlin.de

Opening hours: Daily from 11 am
Products: Individual selection of excitingly presented products
Public transportation: U Kochstraße
Map: No. 23

It's nearly impossible to open a shop in Berlin that's not close to some historic location. In the case of boxoffberlin—or bob, for short—history lies practically at its doorstep. The Berlin Wall ran directly in front of the shop's door. With their combination souvenir shop, café and gallery, bob's founders cater to tourists and locals looking for authentic products from Berlin's creative scene.

Es ist fast unmöglich, einen Laden in Berlin zu eröffnen, der nicht in der Nähe eines geschichtsträchtigen Ortes liegt. Im Falle von boxoffberlin, kurz bob, liegt die Geschichte quasi direkt vor der Tür. Die Berliner Mauer verlief unmittelbar vor der Ladentür. Die bob-Gründer sprechen mit ihrer Mischung aus Souvenirshop, Café und Galerie Touristen und Einheimische an, die authentische Produkte aus der Berliner Kreativszene suchen.

Impossible d'ouvrir un magasin à Berlin sans être à quelques pas d'un endroit chargé d'histoire. Ainsi en est-il de la boutique bob, abrégé de boxoffberlin, où l'histoire est quasiment au pas de la porte. Le Mur de Berlin se dressait autrefois à proximité immédiate. Le large choix d'objets proposés par les fondateurs de cette boutique de souvenirs attire touristes et gens du cru à la recherche de produits authentiques issus de la scène créative berlinoise.

Resulta casi imposible abrir una tienda en Berlín que no esté cerca de un lugar preñado de historia. En el caso de boxoffberlin (también llamado bob), la historia está presente casi frente a la puerta: el Muro de Berlín transcurría frente a los escaparates del local. Los propietarios de bob atraen con su mezcla de tienda de souvenirs, café y galería tanto a turistas como a un público local en busca de genuinos ejemplos de creatividad berlinesa.

DC4 & JOHN DE MAYA PROJECT

Münzstraße 11c
10178 Berlin
Mitte
Phone: +49 / 30 / 28 44 91 99
www.dc4.de

Opening hours: Mon–Sat noon to 8 pm
Products: Designer fashion
Public transportation: U Weinmeisterstraße, Rosa-Luxemburg-Platz
Map: No. 24

This corner shop projects a pure and rough image with the focus on the fashions. If you're looking for cool fashion labels, this is the place: the names on the tags are far from the mainstream. Among other things, you'll find international avant-garde from Japan, Los Angeles, and Copenhagen.

Der Eckladen gibt sich puristisch und rau: der Fokus liegt auf der offerierten Mode. Wer coole Modelabels sucht, ist hier richtig, Namen abseits des Mainstream zieren die Schilder. Im Angebot u. a.: internationale Avantgarde aus Japan, Los Angeles und Kopenhagen.

Un magasin à l'angle de deux rues et aux allures à la fois puristes et primaires : l'accent est mis sur les articles de mode. Celles et ceux qui sont à la recherche de griffes de mode branchées loin des circuits commerciaux habituels ont frappé à la bonne porte. La mode internationale et avant-gardiste du Japon, de Los Angeles et de Copenhague y est notamment proposée.

Ubicado en una esquina, el establecimiento se estila purista y descarnado: la atención hacia la moda que en el local se ofrece. Si va en busca de marcas a la última, ha dado en el clavo: numerosos nombres al margen de las corrientes generales adornan el escaparate. La oferta: moda de vanguardia procedente de Japón, Los Ángeles y Copenhague.

SHOPS . DC4 & JOHN DE MAYA PROJECT   121

Departmentstore Quartier 206

Friedrichstraße 71
10117 Berlin
Mitte
Phone: +49 / 30 / 20 94 68 00
www.departmentstore-quartier206.com

Opening hours: Mon–Fri 11 am to 8 pm, Sat 10 am to 6 pm
Products: Designer fashion, accessories, cosmetics, interiors, bar/café
Public transportation: U Französische Straße, Stadtmitte; S Friedrichstraße
Map: No. 25

Eva Padberg's Special Tip
All the beautiful luxury goods your heart desires, including Manolo Blahnik! Plus, a terrific cosmetics department.

In her shop of superlatives, Anne Maria Jagdfeld brings together everything that's anything in the world of brand names, while never losing her sense of the special and exclusive. Departmentstore marked its tenth anniversary in 2007, and its finely selected range of goods—from fashions and cosmetics to interior furnishings—make comparisons with Barneys New York or Bergdorf Goodman perfectly reasonable.

Anne Maria Jagdfeld vereint in ihrem Ladenkonzept der Superlative alles was Rang und Namen hat in der Welt der Marken, verliert aber dabei nie den Sinn für Besonderes und Exklusives. 2007 feierte der Departmentstore 10-jähriges Bestehen, und mit seinem erlesenen Warenangebot, von Mode über Kosmetik bis hin zu Innenausstattungen, ist ein Vergleich mit Barneys New York oder Bergdorf Goodman durchaus erlaubt.

Anne Maria Jagdfeld réunit dans sa boutique de tous les superlatifs la fine fleur de l'univers des marques, tout en jouant la carte de l'originalité et de l'exclusivité. En 2007, le magasin Departmentstore a fêté ses 10 ans d'existence. Son choix de produits haut de gamme, qu'il s'agisse de mode, de cosmétiques ou de décoration d'intérieur, n'a rien à envier à celui de chez Barneys New York ou encore Bergdorf Goodman.

Anne Maria Jagdfeld reúne en su tienda conceptual de superlativos todo cuanto hay de destacado en el mundo de las marcas, sin perder nunca el olfato para lo especial y exclusivo. El establecimiento celebró en 2007 su décimo aniversario, y su selecta oferta de productos, que van desde la moda y los cosméticos hasta el interiorismo, hace que las comparaciones con Barneys New York o Bergdorf Goodman estén justificadas.

Fiona Bennett Salon

Alte Schönhauser Straße 35
10119 Berlin
Mitte
Phone: +49 / 30 / 28 09 63 30
www.fionabennett.com

Opening hours: By appointment only
Products: Women's, men's and kid's designer hats for day and evening
Public transportation: U Weinmeisterstrasse, Rosa-Luxemburg-Platz; U, S Alexanderplatz, Hackescher Markt
Map: No. 26

Whether for the racetrack, an opera gala, or a film premiere, men and women will find the right piece to grace their heads at Fiona Bennett. Ever since Christina Aguilera wore Fiona Bennett's hats on her world tour, this Berlin hat designer has become a household name. A crowned ram's head shines above the entry sign, and inside the store personally decorated by the proprietor is headwear ranging from the ostentatious to the simple.

Ob für Pferderennen, Opernball oder Filmpremiere ... bei Fiona Bennett finden Frau oder Mann das passende Modell für den Kopf. Spätestens seit Christina Aguilera Fiona Bennetts Hüte bei ihrer Welttournee getragen hat, ist die Berliner Hutdesignerin allseits bekannt. Ein gekrönter Widderkopf prangt über dem Eingangsschild, drinnen, im von ihr persönlich eingerichteten Laden, gibt es Kopfschmuck von pompös bis schlicht.

Quelle que soit l'occasion (course hippique, bal à l'opéra ou film en avant-première...), Elle et Lui trouvent chez Fiona Bennett « chapeau à sa tête ». Notamment depuis que Fiona Bennett a coiffé Christina Aguilera pour sa tournée mondiale, la créatrice de chapeaux berlinoise est devenue une référence mondiale. À l'extérieur, une tête de bélier rehaussée de sa couronne surplombe le panneau à l'entrée, tandis que l'intérieur, aménagé par les soins de Fiona Bennett, abrite des créations aussi bien fastueuses que sobres.

Tanto si es para acudir a una prueba hípica, a la ópera o al estreno de una película, en Fiona Bennett disponen del tocado perfecto para dama y caballero. El espaldarazo definitivo le llegó a la diseñadora de sombreros berlinesa cuando Christina Aguilera lució sus creaciones durante una gira mundial. Una coronada cabeza de carnero adorna el cartel de la entrada; en el local, diseñado personalmente por la propietaria, la oferta de sombreros va desde lo sencillo hasta lo suntuoso.

SHOPS . Fiona Bennett Salon   133

Galeries Lafayette Berlin

Friedrichstraße 76–78
10117 Berlin
Mitte
Phone: +49 / 30 / 20 94 80
www.galerieslafayette.de

Opening hours: Mon–Sat 10 am to 8 pm
Products: Fashion, accessories, body care products, perfumes, delicatessen, French books
Public transportation: U, Bus Französische Straße, Stadtmitte
Map: No. 27

Eva Padberg's Special Tip
This place supplies me with everything I need for that French spirit, and it has the best cheese department in the city.

Since 1996, this glass palace designed by Jean Nouvel exudes French esprit on Friedrichstraße. Ranging over five floors, the only foreign branch of the famous Parisian department store presents the latest in ladies' and men's fashions, accessories, and brand-name cosmetics on the beauty floor. The food court boasts the finest specialties from every region of France: a gourmet paradise!

Seit 1996 versprüht der von Jean Nouvel gestaltete Glaspalast französischen Esprit in der Friedrichstraße. Auf fünf Etagen präsentiert die einzige Auslandsfiliale des bekannten Pariser Kaufhauses aktuelle Damen- und Herrenmode, Accessoires sowie Markenkosmetik in der Beauté-Etage. Im Food-Court findet der Gourmet feinste Spezialitäten aus allen Regionen Frankreichs. Ein Paradies für Schlemmer!

Depuis 1996, le palais de verre dessiné par Jean Nouvel confère à la Friedrichstraße un petit air à la française. L'unique succursale étrangère du célèbre grand magasin parisien présente sur cinq étages les dernières tendances de la mode femme et homme, des accessoires ainsi que des cosmétiques de luxe à l'étage Beauté. Le « Food-Court » propose aux gourmets des spécialités plus exquises les unes que les autres des quatre coins de la France. Un véritable paradis culinaire pour les fines bouches!

El palacio de cristal diseñado por Jean Nouvel insufla desde 1996 cierto esprit francés en la Friedrichstraße. La sucursal en el extranjero de los conocidos grandes almacenes parisinos expone en sus cinco plantas moda masculina y femenina, accesorios y artículos cosméticos en la planta "Beauté". En el área de restauración cuentan con las más deliciosas especialidades de todas las regiones de Francia. Un paraíso para los amigos del buen comer.

Herr von Eden

Alte Schönhauser Straße 14
10119 Berlin
Mitte
Phone: +49 / 30 / 24 04 86 82
www.herrvoneden.com

Opening hours: Mon–Fri 10.30 am to 8 pm, Sat 10 am to 8 pm
Products: Own collection of high-quality suits, shirts, neckties and accessories
Public transportation: U Weinmeisterstraße, Rosa-Luxemburg-Platz
Map: No. 28

Bent Angelo Jensen knows how to dress ladies and gentlemen. The thirty-year-old designer makes men's and women's fashions with a modern dandy look. Classic old-school models with up-to-date cuts are his recipe for success. From garishly striped shirts with exquisite details to Marlene Dietrich-style pantsuits, a modern fit and precision workmanship make every outfit an attention-getter.

Bent Angelo Jensen weiß wie man Ladies und Gentlemen kleidet. Der 30-Jährige macht Mode im modernen Dandy Look für Sie und Ihn. Klassische Modelle der alten Schule mit aktuellen Schnitten sind das Erfolgskonzept. Ob grell gestreifte Hemden mit raffinierten Details oder ein Hosenanzug im Marlene-Dietrich-Stil, moderne Passformen und präzise Verarbeitung machen jedes Outfit zu einem Hingucker.

Bent Angelo Jensen sait comment habiller Ladies et Gentlemen. Ce styliste âgé de 30 ans propose une collection style dandy moderne pour Elle et pour Lui. Le secret de sa réussite ? Des modèles classiques de la vieille école aux coupes tendance. Chemises à rayures vives et aux détails raffinés ou encore tailleur-pantalon façon Marlène Dietrich, les lignes modernes et la finition précise de chacune des tenues ne peuvent qu'attirer tous les regards.

Bent Angelo Jensen sabe como vestir a la dama y el caballero, y a sus 30 años diseña modelos muy próximos al dandy para él y para ella. Su éxito se basa en la actualización con cortes modernos de modelos clásicos de la vieja escuela. Tanto si se trata de camisas a rayas con detalles exclusivos o de un traje de chaqueta y pantalón al estilo de Marlene Dietrich, la modernidad de las líneas y la exquisita confección hacen de cada modelo una prenda irresistible.

lucid21

Christinenstraße 26
10119 Berlin
Prenzlauer Berg
Phone: +49 / 30 / 62 98 16 52
www.lucid21.net

Opening hours: Tue–Fri noon to 7 pm, Sat noon to 4 pm
Products: Women's fashion, jewelry, accessories
Public transportation: U Senefelderplatz
Map: No. 29

This "mini flagship store" of designers and businessmen Luis Gunsch and Stefan Münzenmaier is both shop and showroom. They call their style "comfortable romantic minimalism." Skillful use of feminine cuts and graphic details make the collections timeless and suitable for young and old alike. Each item is a piece of home that you can wear.

Der „Miniflagshipstore" der Designer und Unternehmer Luis Gunsch und Stefan Münzenmaier ist Showroom und Laden in einem. Sie selbst nennen ihren Stil „romantischen Minimalismus zum Wohlfühlen". Gekonnter Umgang mit femininen Schnitten und grafischen Details machen die Kollektionen zeitlos und tragbar für Jung und Alt. Jedes Modell ist ein Stück Heimatgefühl zum Anziehen.

Le « magasin porte-drapeau » des créateurs de mode et entrepreneurs Luis Gunsch et Stefan Münzenmaier fait à la fois office de salle d'exposition et de boutique. Eux-mêmes qualifient leur style de « minimalisme romantique au service du bien-être ». La maîtrise parfaite des coupes féminines et les détails graphiques rendent les collections intemporelles et siéent à tous les âges. Chaque modèle offre une véritable sensation de seconde peau.

El "miniedificio insignia" de los diseñadores y empresarios Luis Gunsch y Stefan Münzenmaier sirve a un tiempo de sala de exhibición y punto de venta. Los propietarios definen su estilo como "minimalismo romántico para sentirse bien" . Su talento a la hora de crear cortes femeninos y detalles gráficos dotan de un enorme clasicismo a sus creaciones y las hacen apropiadas para todas las edades. Cada modelo es un retazo de hogar que lucir orgulloso.

Mercedes-Benz Gallery

Unter den Linden 14
10117 Berlin
Mitte
Phone: +49 / 30 / 39 01 81 00
www.berlin.mercedes-benz.com

Opening hours: Daily 9 am to 10 pm
Public transportation: U Französische Straße; U, S Brandenburger Tor, Friedrichstraße
Map: No. 30

Just a few steps from where history began for the Mercedes-Benz Berlin branch in 1909, the Mercedes-Benz Gallery brings the myth of the brand with the star to life in all its facets. With a fascinating design plan and innovative media technologies, the exclusive atmosphere of the over 16,000 sq. ft. of exhibition space on the Unter den Linden boulevard sets groundbreaking standards of brand presentation.

Nur wenige Meter von der Stelle entfernt, an der die Historie der Mercedes-Benz Niederlassung Berlin 1909 ihren Anfang nahm, macht die Mercedes-Benz Gallery den Mythos der Marke mit dem Stern in all seinen Facetten erlebbar. Mit einem faszinierenden Raum- und Gestaltungskonzept und der Einbindung innovativer Medientechnik setzt die Ausstellungsfläche mit ihrem exklusiven Ambiente auf über 1.500 m² am Prachtboulevard Unter den Linden wegweisende Standards in der Markenpräsentation.

A quelques mètres de l'endroit où naquit en 1909 l'histoire de la succursale Mercedes-Benz de Berlin, la Mercedes-Benz Gallery permet au visiteur de toucher du doigt le mythe de la marque à l'étoile et ses multiples facettes. Grâce à une conception fascinante en matière d'espace et d'aménagement et à une intégration réussie de techniques médiatiques innovatrices, la surface d'exposition et l'ambiance exclusive qu'on y respire sur plus de 1500 m² le long du magnifique boulevard Unter den Linden, instaurent là, dans la présentation de marque, des standards de qualité promis à un bel avenir.

A escasos metros del lugar en el que en 1909 comenzara la historia de la sucursal de Mercedes-Benz en Berlín, la Mercedes-Benz Gallery acerca al gran público el mito de la marca de la estrella. El fascinante diseño y concepción espacial y la integración de innovadoras técnicas audiovisuales contribuyen a que el exclusivo ambiente que destilan los 1.500 m² de exposición en la noble avenida Unter den Linden marque el camino a seguir en la presentación de la marca.

Qualität von Mercedes-Benz.

MYKITA

Rosa-Luxemburg-Straße 6
10178 Berlin
Mitte
Phone: +49 / 30 / 67 30 87 15
www.mykita.com

Opening hours: Mon–Fri 11 am to 8 pm, Sat noon to 6 pm
Products: Designer eyewear
Public transportation: U, S Alexanderplatz
Map: No. 31

Designer eyewear: Made in Berlin. This futuristic store brings to mind a white cube—the interior is spare and functional, perfectly complementing the design of the glasses. All models are held just by a clever connection system, with no screws at all. Thanks to their high standard of craftsmanship and modern design, Mykita glasses are also popular with international stars.

Designerbrillen, „handmade in Berlin". Der futuristische Laden erinnert an einen weissen Würfel, ist schlicht und funktional eingerichtet und passt optimal zum Design der Brillen. Alle Modelle halten durch ein patentiertes Federgelenk und kommen ganz ohne Schrauben aus. Hochwertige Verarbeitung und modernes Design machen Mykita-Brillen auch bei internationalen Stars beliebt.

Lunettes design « made in Berlin ». Associant sobriété et fonctionnalité, cette boutique futuriste fait penser à un dé blanc et s'accorde parfaitement au design des lunettes. Les modèles tiennent tous grâce à un ingénieux système d'emboîtement lequel rend les vis superflues. La qualité de finition supérieure et la modernité du design font le succès des lunettes Mykita que même les stars internationales aiment porter.

Gafas de diseño «made in Berlin». El futurista local, de diseño sencillo y funcional, recuerda en sus formas un dado blanco y complementa perfectamente el diseño de las gafas. Las gafas están construidas con un ingenioso sistema de enganches que hace innecesarios los tornillos. La extraordinaria calidad y el moderno diseño de las gafas de Mykita las ha hecho muy populares entre las estrellas internacionales.

NANNA KUCKUCK – Haute Couture

Bleibtreustraße 52
10623 Berlin
Charlottenburg
Phone: +49 / 30 / 31 50 71 50
www.nanna-kuckuck.com

Opening hours: Tue–Fri noon to 7 pm, Sat noon to 4 pm
Products: Haute couture, glamorous dresses, unique draped gowns
Public transportation: S Savignyplatz
Map: No. 32

Tita von Hardenberg's Special Tip
Here you can unabashedly live out your innermost princess dreams. Wonderfully opulent gowns are made of fabrics that Nanna herself discovered in the farthest corners of the world.

Nanna Kuckuck has been a fixture in Berlin's fashion scene for years. Following individual consulting in the showroom, precious silks and brocades are crafted into tailor-made, one-off creations beloved by fashion-conscious clients and celebrities. Inspired by Kuckuck's travels to the Near and Far East, her glamorous evening gowns are a colorful alternative to the little black dress.

In der Berliner Modeszene ist Nanna Kuckuck schon seit Jahren eine feste Größe. Nach individueller Beratung im Showroom werden edle Seidenstoffe und Brokate zu maßgefertigten Unikaten verarbeitet, die bei modebewussten Kundinnen und prominenten Damen beliebt sind. Inspiriert von Kuckucks Orient und Asien Reisen, sind die glamourösen Abendroben eine farbenfrohe Alternative zum Kleinen Schwarzen.

Des années déjà que Nanna Kuckuck est une grande pointure de l'univers de la haute couture berlinoise. Accueil et conseils personnalisés en boutique avant que les étoffes précieuses telles que soie et brocarts ne soient taillées en pièces uniques sur mesure, rencontrant un véritable succès auprès de clientes attentives à leur image et de célébrités féminines. Inspirées des multiples voyages de N. Kuckuck en Orient et en Asie, les glamoureuses robes de soirée sont une alternative colorée aux petites robes noires.

Nanna Kuckuck es desde hace años una de las grandes en el mundillo berlinés de la moda. Tras la atención personal en el showroom, comienza el proceso de confección de modelos únicos con las nobles sedas y brocados tan del gusto de su clientela, repleta de rostros famosos y dotada de gran sentido de la moda. Inspirada en los viajes que Kuckuck realiza por Asia y Oriente, sus trajes de gala ofrecen una colorista alternativa al clásico vestido negro.

RENÉ LEZARD Shop Berlin Mitte

Alte Schönhauser Straße 42
10119 Berlin
Mitte
Phone: +49 / 30 / 28 04 06 66
www.rene-lezard.com

Opening hours: Mon–Sat 11 am to 8 pm
Products: Designer fashion, accessories
Public transportation: U Weinmeisterstraße, Rosa-Luxemburg-Platz
Map: No. 33

RENÉ LEZARD is an exclusive fashion brand for ladies and gentlemen in the premium segment. It stands for confident individuality, unmistakable design, and uncompromising quality in materials and workmanship. The design of the Berlin shop captivates the eye with clear lines combined with classic designs. Studio spots cast the casual, elegant fashions and accessories in a suitable light.

RENÉ LEZARD ist eine exklusive Modemarke für Damen und Herren im Premium-Segment. Sie steht für selbstbewußte Individualität, unverwechselbares Design und kompromisslose Qualität bei Material und Verarbeitung. Die Einrichtung des Shops in Berlin besticht durch klare Linien kombiniert mit Design Klassikern. Studio-Spots setzten die leger elegante Mode und Accessoires ins passende Licht.

RENÉ LEZARD est une marque exclusive de prêt-à-porter prisée par les femmes et les hommes affichant une certaine aisance. Une marque synonyme d'individualité sans complexe, d'un design unique en son genre et d'une qualité intransigeante aussi bien au niveau des matières que de la confection. L'aménagement de la boutique berlinoise se distingue par des lignes épurées associées à un design classique. Des projecteurs mettent parfaitement en lumière articles de mode et accessoires à la fois élégants et décontractés.

RENÉ LEZARD es una exclusiva marca de moda masculina y femenina de gama muy alta. Su nombre es sinónimo de individualidad, inconfundible diseño y máxima calidad en los materiales y la confección. El interiorismo de la tienda berlinesa se caracteriza por la claridad de líneas, combinada con clásicos del diseño. Los focos de estudio subrayan con la mejor de las luces el estilo desenfadado y elegante de prendas y accesorios.

rooms interior GmbH

Leipziger Straße 112
10117 Berlin
Mitte
Phone: +49 / 30 / 20 67 38 33
www.rooms-interior.de

Opening hours: Mon–Fri 11 am to 8 pm, Sat 11 am to 6 pm
Products: Furniture
Public transportation: U Stadtmitte
Map: No. 34

In his mid-thirties, Stefan Schad is one of the "young wild ones" of the furniture and interior design world. After a rocket-propelled career in the fashion industry, he made a name for himself as an interior designer, opening "rooms interior" in 2006. You'll find everything here, from an individual design object to complete home furnishings. On request, Schad will personally design your apartment, office, or shop.

Stefan Schad gehört mit Mitte Dreißig zu den „jungen Wilden" der Möbel- und Einrichtungsszene. Nach einer steilen Karriere in der Modebranche, machte er sich einen Namen als Interiordesigner und eröffnete 2006 „rooms interior". Hier findet man alles, vom einzelnen Designobjekt bis hin zur kompletten Wohnungsausstattung. Auf Wunsch gestaltet Schad persönlich Privatwohnung, Büro oder Laden.

Stefan Schad, dans les trente-cinq ans, compte parmi les « jeunes indomptables » de l'univers du mobilier et de l'aménagement. Après une carrière fulgurante dans le monde de la mode, il réussit à se faire un nom en tant que décorateur d'intérieur et ouvre en 2006 « rooms interior ». Une boutique où l'on trouve de tout, de l'article design unique jusqu'à l'ameublement complet. Aménagement personnalisé d'appartement privé, de bureau ou de magasin sur demande.

A sus treinta y pocos años, Stefan Schad se cuenta entre los enfants terribles del diseño de muebles e interiores. Tras una meteórica carrera en el sector de la moda empezó a labrarse un nombre como interiorista y en 2006 abrió "rooms interior". Aquí encontraremos de todo, desde objetos individuales de diseño hasta conceptos integrales para la vivienda. Schad acepta también encargos para ocuparse personalmente de la decoración de viviendas privadas, despachos y locales.

SHAN RAHIMKHAN

Am Gendarmenmarkt
Markgrafenstraße 36
10117 Berlin
Mitte
Phone: +49 / 30 / 2 06 78 90
www.shanrahimkhan.de

Opening hours: CASA: Mon–Fri 10 am to 8 pm, Sat 10 am to 6 pm; COIFFEUR: Mon–Fri 9 am
to 7 pm; CAFE: Mon–Sat 8 am to midnight, Sun 10 am to 10 pm
Products: CASA, COIFFEUR, CAFE
Public transportation: U Hausvogteiplatz
Map: No. 35

Two majestic peacocks form the emblem beneath which reads "SHAN RAHIMKHAN—CASA, COIFFEUR,
CAFE." Originally from Tehran, the celebrity hairstylist has built a style empire at Gendarmenmarkt.
After a well-heeled client has been styled by the team or is finished relaxing in the tastefully appointed
café, he or she can pick out a suitable home accessory in the adjoining boutique.

Zwei majestätische Pfauen bilden das Wappen, darunter liest man Shan Rahimkhan CASA, COIFFEUR,
CAFE. Der aus Teheran stammende Promifriseur hat am Gendarmenmarkt ein Stil-Imperium errichtet.
Nachdem sich der betuchte Kunde vom Team hat stylen lassen, oder im stilvollen Café entspannt hat,
kann Er oder Sie aus der angeschlossenen Boutique das passende Wohnaccessoire mit nach Hause
nehmen.

Deux paons majestueux forment les armoiries au-dessous desquelles on peut lire Shan Rahimkhan
CASA, COIFFEUR, CAFE. Le coiffeur de renom originaire de Téhéran a bâti un véritable empire au style
particulier sur la place du Gendarmenmarkt. Après avoir confié ses cheveux à l'équipe de profession-
nels ou bien s'être détendu dans le café sélect, le client huppé peut ensuite flâner dans la boutique
adjacente à la recherche de l'accessoire de décoration de son choix.

Dos majestuosos pavos reales adornan el emblema del local, bajo el que puede leerse "Shan
Rahimkhan CASA, COIFFEUR, CAFE" . El peluquero de los famosos, oriundo de Teherán, ha estableci-
do su imperio del estilo en el Gendarmenmarkt. Una vez ha pasado por las manos del equipo de pelu-
quería, o después quizá de relajarse en el café, el acomodado cliente puede visitar la tienda contigua y
llevarse a casa algún accesorio doméstico.

Vintage-Sunglasses.de + OptiKing

Eberswalder Straße 34
10437 Berlin
Prenzlauer Berg
Phone: +49 / 30 / 47 37 24 88
www.vintage-sunglasses-shop.de, www.optiking.de

Opening hours: Nov–Feb Mon–Sat noon to 6 pm and Mar–Oct Mon–Sat noon to 8 pm
Products: Original sunglasses and frames of the '70s, '80s, and '90s
Public transportation: U Eberswalder Straße
Map: No. 36

If you want to protect your eyes from sunlight or lightning storms with originals from the '70s, '80s, or '90s, you should pay a visit to Carsten Dennhardt's shop in the Prenzlauer Berg district, where the motto is "100-Percent Vintage, Nothing Retro!" Each piece on offer has never been worn, and the friendly service of the personable shop owner guarantees a pleasant shopping experience. The celebrity database at Vintage-Sunglasses.de shows what shades were worn by various stars.

Wer seine Augen mit Originalen aus den 70er-, 80er- oder 90er-Jahren vor Sonne oder Blitzlichtgewitter schützen will, sollte Carsten Dennhardts Laden am Prenzlauer Berg einen Besuch abstatten. „100 Prozent Vintage, kein Retro!", lautet das Motto; jedes angebotene Modell ist „neu" aus Altbeständen und garantiert ungetragen. Eine Celebrity-Datenbank zeigt, welche Brille welcher Star getragen hat.

Pour protéger ses yeux du soleil ou du crépitement des flashs avec des lunettes cultes des années 70, 80 ou 90, une seule adresse : la boutique de Carsten Dennhardt dans le quartier de Prenzlauer Berg. « 100% vintage, aucunement rétro ! », telle est sa devise. L'ensemble des modèles proposés est neuf et le propriétaire du magasin, à l'entière disposition de ses clients, réserve un accueil sympathique. Une base de données spéciale Célébrités peut également être consultée sur Vintage-Sunglasses.de, dans laquelle sont répertoriées les lunettes portées par différentes stars.

Para proteger los ojos del sol o el resplandor de los flashes con modelos originales de los años 70, 80 y 90, nada como una visita al local de Carsten Dennhardt en Prenzlauer Berg. "¡Cien por cien vintage, nada de retro!" , es su lema. Todos los modelos en oferta son de primera mano, y el amable personal de la tienda garantiza que la compra será una experiencia muy agradable. La agenda de famosos de Vintage-Sunglasses.de recoge qué estrellas lucieron qué modelo.

HIGHLIGHTS

BADESCHIFF an der arena Berlin

Eichenstraße 4
12435 Berlin
Treptow
Phone: +49 / 178 / 9 50 01 63
www.badeschiff.de

Opening hours: Summer season daily 8 am to open end, winter season Mon+Fri noon to 3 am, Tue+Thu noon to midnight, Wed+Sun 10 am to midnight, Sat 10 am to 3 am
Public transportation: U Schlesisches Tor; S Treptower Park
Map: No. 37

Swimming pool in summer, sauna in winter—in the middle of the River Spree and with a panoramic view, to boot! The futuristic version of a traditional German river swimming area was developed as part of a competition. The award-winning Badeschiff ("swimming ship") has room for swimming and sunbathing on three floating boardwalks—until winter comes along and the whole affair is converted into a giant sauna using a wood and high-tech bubble construction.

Im Sommer schwimmen, im Winter saunieren – mitten auf der Spree, Panoramablick inklusive. Die futuristische Version eines traditionellen Flussschwimmbades wurde im Rahmen eines Wettbewerbes entwickelt. Das preisgekrönte Badeschiff bietet auf zwei Holzstegen sowie in einem schwimmenden Pool Platz zum Baden und Sonnen, bis es im Winter mit Hilfe einer Konstruktion aus Holz und High-Tec-Folie zu einer Saunalandschaft umfunktioniert wird.

Piscine en été, sauna en hiver – au beau milieu de la Spree, avec vue panoramique. La version futuriste d'une piscine traditionnelle alimentée par l'eau de rivière vit le jour dans le cadre d'un concours. Le Badeschiff (littéralement bateau-baignoire) primé, constitué de trois pontons flottants en bois, offre la possibilité de se baigner en plein air et de lézarder au soleil, avant de se transformer en hiver en espace sauna recouvert d'une construction en bois et d'une bulle haute technologie.

Piscina en verano y sauna en invierno, en pleno Spree y con buenas vistas. La futurista versión de una piscina fluvial surgió de un concurso. La galardonada "barcaza de baño" (Badeschiff) consta de tres entarimados y una piscina en los que refrescarse y tomar el sol. En invierno, la piscina se convierte en sauna con la ayuda de una estructura de madera y una cubierta flexible de alta tecnología.

Berliner Ensemble

Bertolt-Brecht-Platz 1
10117 Berlin
Mitte
Phone: +49 / 30 / 28 40 81 55
www.berliner-ensemble.de

Opening hours: Box office Mon–Fri 8 am to 6 pm, Sat+Sun and public holidays 11 am to 6 pm
Public transportation: U, S, Bus, Tram Friedrichstraße, Oranienburgerstraße
Map: No. 38

When it was founded by Bertolt Brecht in 1949, the Berliner Ensemble or "BE" was a community of actors that included Ernst Busch and Brecht's wife Helene Weigel. Such plays as "Mother Courage and Her Children" and "The Threepenny Opera" premiered here. Today, with Picasso's peace dove as its emblem, the theater is one of the leading stages in the German-speaking world.

Bei seiner Gründung durch Bertolt Brecht 1949 war das Berliner Ensemble, kurz BE, eine Gemeinschaft von Schauspielern, zu der u. a. Ernst Busch und Brechts Frau Helene Weigel gehörten. Stücke wie „Mutter Courage und ihre Kinder" und „Die Dreigroschenoper" feierten hier ihre Uraufführung. Heute ist das Theater mit Picassos Friedenstaube als Wahrzeichen eine der führenden deutschsprachigen Bühnen.

Lors de sa création par Bertolt Brecht en 1949, le Berliner Ensemble (BE) était au départ une compagnie théâtrale constituée de plusieurs comédiens, dont Ernst Busch et Helene Weigel, épouse de Brecht. Les premières représentations des pièces telles que « Mère Courage et ses enfants » et « l'Opéra de quat'sous » ont été données en ces lieux. Aujourd'hui, le bâtiment, sous l'emblème de la colombe de la paix de Picasso, est l'un des théâtres de langue allemande les plus réputés.

Cuando Bertolt Brecht fundó el Berliner Ensemble (BE), éste consistía en una comunidad de actores entre los que se contaban Ernst Busch y Helene Weigel, la mujer de Brecht. Aquí se estrenaron piezas como "Madre Coraje y sus hijos" o "La ópera de tres peniques". En la actualidad, el teatro (que ha adoptado como símbolo la picassiana paloma de la paz) es uno de los principales escenarios de Alemania.

Galerie CAMERA WORK

Kantstraße 149
10623 Berlin
Charlottenburg
Phone: +49 / 30 / 3 10 07 73
www.camerawork.de

Opening hours: Tue–Sat 11 am to 6 pm
Public transportation: U Uhlandstraße; S Savignyplatz
Map: No. 39

Tita von Hardenberg's Special Tip

Here is a fine selection of the best photographers in the world—and some who are on their way to becoming one of the best. The opening receptions are renowned and sometimes go on until morning.

Founded in 1997 and named after Alfred Stieglitz's legendary magazine "Camera Work," this gallery focuses not only on such icons of photography as Helmut Newton, Richard Avedon, Irving Penn, and Man Ray, but also on young artists just starting out in their careers. Consider Ralph Mecke, for instance, or Martin Schoeller, both of whom had their first German exhibitions at CAMERA WORK and have since followed paths of impressive artistic development.

Die 1997 gegründete und nach Alfred Stieglitz' legendärer Zeitschrift „Camera Work" benannte Galerie legt ihren Fokus nicht nur auf die Ikonen der Fotografie wie Helmut Newton, Richard Avedon, Irving Penn oder Man Ray, sondern auch auf junge, am Beginn ihrer Karriere stehende Künstler. Hier sind beispielhaft Ralph Mecke oder Martin Schoeller zu nennen, die ihre jeweils erste Ausstellung in Deutschland bei CAMERA WORK hatten und seitdem eine beeindruckende künstlerische Entwicklung beschritten haben.

Baptisée ainsi en hommage à la légendaire revue « Camera Work » éditée par Alfred Stieglitz, la galerie fondée en 1997 réunit des œuvres non seulement d'icônes de la photographie telles que Helmut Newton, Richard Avedon, Irving Penn ou Man Ray, mais aussi de jeunes artistes débutants. Citons à titre d'exemple Ralph Mecke ou encore Martin Schoeller, qui ont tous deux présenté leur première exposition en Allemagne dans les locaux de la Camera Work et qui ont depuis embrassé une prestigieuse carrière artistique.

La galería, fundada en 1997 y bautizada con el nombre del legendario periódico de Alfred Stieglitz, se concentra no sólo en iconos de la fotografía como Helmut Newton, Richard Avedon, Irving Penn o Man Ray, sino también en artistas jóvenes en los albores de su carrera. Cabe mencionar a modo de ejemplo a Ralph Mecke y Martin Schoeller: ambos presentaron su primera exposición en Alemania en CAMERA WORK y han demostrado posteriormente una impresionante progresión artística.

East Side Gallery

Mühlenstraße 1
10243 Berlin
Friedrichshain

Public transportation: U, S Warschauer Straße; S Ostbahnhof
Map: No. 40

The Wall separated West Berlin from East Berlin for over twenty-eight years. On the longest preserved piece of the Wall, the largest open-air gallery in the world was created in February 1990. Coming from 21 countries, 118 artists painted the originally white and gray wall, creating an international monument to freedom on the 1,500-yard section running along the River Spree.

Mehr als 28 Jahre trennte die Mauer West- von Ostberlin. Am längsten erhaltenen Stück der Mauer entstand im Februar 1990 die größte Open-Air-Galerie der Welt. Auf dem 1,4 Kilometer langen Abschnitt entlang der Spree haben 118 Künstler aus 21 Ländern die früher weiß-graue Mauer bemalt und so ein internationales Denkmal für die Freiheit geschaffen.

Durant plus de 28 années, le Mur séparera Berlin-Ouest de Berlin-Est. En février 1990, la plus grande galerie d'art à ciel ouvert du monde s'installe en bordure de la plus longue section restante du mur. 118 artistes venus de 21 pays différents se sont donnés rendez-vous le long de la Spree pour décorer de fresques les vestiges du mur (sur 1,4 kilomètres) autrefois gris terne. Un monument international qui incarne l'aspiration à la liberté.

El Muro dividió Berlín en dos partes durante más de 28 años. Junto al fragmento más largo que se conserva de aquel se instaló en febrero de 1990 la mayor galería al aire libre del mundo. A lo largo de 1.400 metros, a orillas del Spree, 118 artistas de 21 países transformaron el otrora blanco grisáceo del muro en un monumento internacional a la libertad.

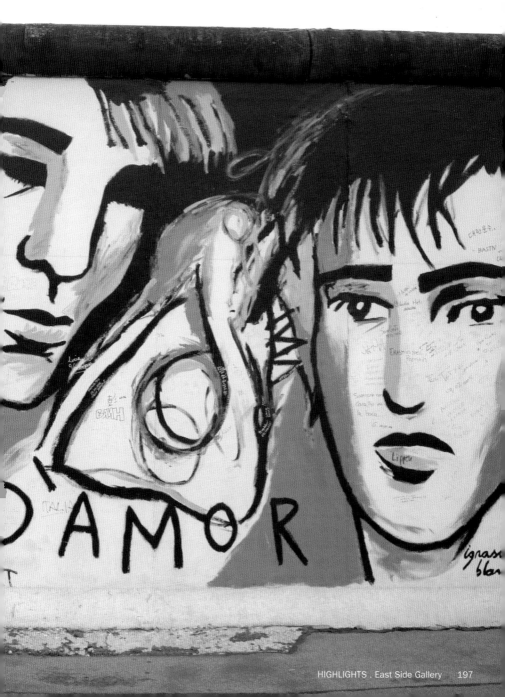

Hackescher Markt

Hackescher Markt 1
10178 Berlin
Mitte

Public transportation: S Hackescher Markt
Map: No. 41

Eva Padberg's Special Tip
This is my favorite place to stroll around: interesting small shops that don't conform to mass tastes.

In the early 19th century, Town Major Hans C. F. Graf von Hacke ordered the creation of the plaza on what was previously swampland. Since then, Hackescher Markt developed first into a public transit hub and later into the departure point to the surrounding district with its countless shops, restaurants, and clubs, as well as the Hackesche Höfe complex, Lustgarten park, Berlin Cathedral, and Museum Island.

Anfang des 19. Jahrhunderts ließ der Berliner Stadtkommandant Hans C. F. Graf von Hacke den Platz auf ehemaligem Sumpfland errichten. Seitdem entwickelte sich der Hackesche Markt erst zum Knotenpunkt des öffentlichen Verkehrs und später zum Ausgangspunkt in das umliegende Viertel mit unzähligen Shops, Restaurants und Clubs sowie zu den Hackesche Höfen, dem Lustgarten, dem Berliner Dom oder der Museumsinsel.

Hans C. F. Graf von Hacke, commandant de la ville de Berlin, fit construire la place au début du 19ème siècle sur un ancien terrain marécageux. Depuis, le Hackescher Markt a tout d'abord joué le rôle de plaque tournante du réseau de transport public, avant de constituer par la suite le point de départ pour découvrir le quartier environnant avec ses innombrables boutiques, restaurants et clubs ainsi que les Hackesche Höfen (ensemble de cours), le Lustgarten (jardin d'agrément), le Berliner Dom (cathédrale de Berlin) ou encore la Museumsinsel (Île aux musées).

A comienzos del siglo XIX, Hans C. F. Graf von Hacke, a la sazón comandante de la ciudad, ordenó la construcción de esta plaza en una antigua ciénaga. Con el tiempo, la plaza se convirtió primero en eje principal del transporte público y más tarde en punto de acceso al barrio circundante y sus innumerables tiendas, restaurantes y clubs, así como a los Hackesche Höfe, el Lustgarten, la catedral de Berlín y la Isla de los Museos.

Kino International

Karl-Marx-Allee 33
10178 Berlin
Mitte
Phone: +49 / 30 / 24 75 60 11
www.yorck.de

Opening hours: Variable
Public transportation: U Schillingstraße; U, S Alexanderplatz
Map: No. 42

Tita von Hardenberg's Special Tip
Every cinema should look like this: chandeliers in the foyer, plush armchairs in the bar. This is one of the finest examples of East German modern design and an architectural experience.

In a time of multiplex cinemas and big screen televisions, the "Inter," as it's fondly called, brings back memories of a past age of large motion picture houses. Constructed during East Germany's Honecker era and built in the style of the '60s, it served as the premier cinema of the GDR until 1989. Today, visitors admire its unique atmosphere. Each year, the cinema plays host to the Berlin International Film Festival.

In Zeiten von Multiplexkinos und Großbildfernsehern ist das „Inter" eine Reminiszenz an die vergangene Zeit großer Lichtspieltheater. Erbaut in der Ära Honecker und im Stil der 60er-Jahre eingerichtet, diente das Haus bis 1989 als Premierenkino der DDR. Heute schätzen seine Besucher die besondere Atmosphäre. Das Haus ist alljährlich Spielstätte der Berlinale.

Dans la société actuelle où cinémas multiplex et téléviseurs à écran géant font fureur, l'« Inter » est une réminiscence des grands cinémas d'autrefois. Construit au cours de l'ère Honecker et aménagé dans le style des années 60, l'édifice a jusqu'en 1989 fait office de cinéma de l'ancienne RDA réservé aux avant-premières. Aujourd'hui, les spectateurs savent apprécier à sa juste valeur l'atmosphère si particulière. Le bâtiment accueille tous les ans la Berlinale (Festival international du film de Berlin).

En esta época de cines multiplex y televisores gigantes, el cine Inter es casi una reliquia de otros tiempos. Construido en la era Honecker y equipado según el gusto de los años sesenta, hasta 1989 sirvió como sala de estreno en la RDA. En la actualidad, los clientes aprecian su inimitable atmósfera. Año tras año, el cine acoge la Berlinale.

Mercedes-Benz Fashion Week Berlin

Bebelplatz
10117 Berlin
Mitte
www.mercedes-benzfashionweek.com

Date: Spring and summer, access to shows by invitation only
Public transportation: U Französische Straße; U, S Friedrichstraße
Map: No. 43

Since its inception in 2007, the Mercedes-Benz Berlin Fashion Week has taken a firm position among the top five of the world's most important fashion events. The unique combination of young talent and established names in fashion—with a high percentage of German designers—gives the event (held in January and July) its own flavor, to the thrill of a worldwide audience.

Nach ihrem Start in 2007 hat sich die Mercedes-Benz Fashion Week Berlin einen festen Platz unter den Top 5 der weltweit wichtigsten Modeveranstaltungen sichern können. Die einzigartige Mischung aus jungen Talenten und etablierten Modegrößen sowie der hohe Anteil deutscher Designer geben der im Januar und Juli stattfindenden Veranstaltung ihr eigenes Profil und begeistert damit ein weltweites Publikum.

Lancée en 2007, la Mercedes-Benz Fashion Week Berlin est devenue un rendez-vous incontournable et fait désormais partie du top 5 des spectacles de mode les plus importants au monde. Réunissant sous un même toit des jeunes talents et des artistes chevronnés avec un pourcentage élevé de créateurs allemands, cet évènement qui a lieu en janvier et en juillet ne manque pas de relief et attire logiquement un public international, pour ne pas dire intercontinental.

Desde su arranque en 2007, la Mercedes-Benz Fashion Week Berlin se ha asegurado un puesto entre los 5 principales acontecimientos de la moda a escala mundial. En enero y julio de cada año se produce una combinación única de jóvenes talentos y grandes nombres de la costura, entre ellos un elevado porcentaje de diseñadores alemanes, que dota al evento de un perfil propio y encandila al público internacional.

Other titles by teNeues

ISBN 978-3-8327-9309-8

ISBN 978-3-8327-9274-9

ISBN 978-3-8327-9398-2

ISBN 978-3-8327-9237-4

ISBN 978-3-8327-9247-3

ISBN 978-3-8327-9234-3

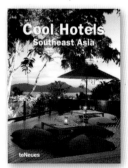

ISBN 978-3-8327-9308-1

ISBN 978-3-8327-9243-5

ISBN 978-3-8327-9230-5

Size: **14.3 x 18.5 cm**, 5⅝ x 7¼ in., 224 pp., **Flexicover**, c. 200 color photographs
Text: English / German / French / Spanish / Italian
www.teneues.com

Other titles by teNeues

ISBN 978-3-8327-9248-0

ISBN 978-3-8327-9396-8

ISBN 978-3-8327-9399-9

ISBN 978-3-8327-9323-4

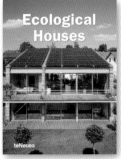

ISBN 978-3-8327-9227-5

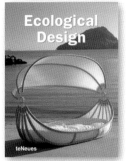

ISBN 978-3-8327-9229-9

ISBN 978-3-8327-9228-2

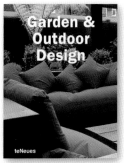

ISBN 978-3-8327-9307-4

ISBN 978-3-8327-9338-8

Size: **14.3 x 18.5 cm**, 5⅝ x 7¼ in., 224 pp., **Flexicover**, c. 200 color photographs
Text: English / German / French / Spanish / Italian
www.teneues.com

Other titles by teNeues

ISBN 978-3-8327-9236-7

ISBN 978-3-8327-9202-2

ISBN 978-3-8327-9400-2

ISBN 978-3-8327-9293-0

ISBN 978-3-8327-9294-7

ISBN 978-3-8327-9295-4

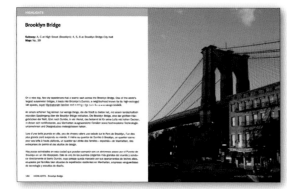

Interior Pages
Cool Guide New York

Size: **14.3 x 18.5 cm**, 5⅝ x 7¼ in., 224 pp., **Flexicover**, c. 200 color photographs
Text: English / German / French / Spanish
www.teneues.com